P9-CDE-479

Healing
Bodies and Souls

A Practical Guide for Congregations

W. Daniel Hale and
Harold G. Koenig

FORTRESS PRESS
Minneapolis

AIF free
11/03

HEALING BODIES AND SOULS
A Practical Guide for Congregations

Copyright © 2003 Augsburg Fortress. All rights reserved. Except for brief quotations in critical articles or reviews, no part of this book may be reproduced in any manner without prior written permission from the publisher. Write: Permissions, Augsburg Fortress, Box 1209, Minneapolis, MN 55440.

Scripture quotations from the New Revised Standard Version of the Bible are copyright © 1989 by the Division of Christian Education of the National Council of the Churches of Christ in the United States of America and are used by permission.

Cover image: "Teamwork" © D. M. Grethen/Images.com. Used by permission.
Cover design: Marti Naughton
Book design: Ann Delgehausen

ISBN: 0-8006-3629-5

The paper used in this publication meets the minimum requirements of American National Standard for Information Sciences—Permanence of Paper for Printed Library Materials, ANSI Z329.48-1984.

Manufactured in the U.S.A.
07   06   05   04   03   1   2   3   4   5   6   7   8   9   10

Healing Bodies and Souls

Praise for Healing Bodies and Souls

"*Sparkling, smart, and practical,* Healing Bodies and Souls *is filled with integrity and compassion. This book not only describes but models the rich interplay between medical intelligence and whole-life human development. Although rooted in their deep competence in gerontology, Hale and Koenig sketch a way toward congregations that are vital and life-giving for the whole lifespan. Congregations that follow Hale and Koenig's lead are going to find their future in these life-giving ministries.*"

—Gary Gundersen
Director, Interfaith Health Program
Rollins School of Public Health, Emory University

"*So much of health and healing is about education and self-care, and those needs are not being met by the current system of health care. Meeting those needs is the work of the church and the members of the body of Christ—a way to put faith into action. This book tells stories that inspire and gives the basic guidelines for putting one's faith into action.*"

—Gwen W. Halaas, M.D.
Director, Ministerial Health and Wellness,
Evangelical Lutheran Church in America

"*The precious gift of healthy life is among the most important of Christian values. W. Daniel Hale and Harold G. Koenig are uniquely qualified in highlighting all the practical ways in which church communities can enhance the health of those in their midst and, by example, of all those who share in our common humanity.*"

—Stephen G. Post
Professor of Bioethics and Religion
School of Medicine, Case Western Reserve University

To Julie and Bill O'Neill

With heartfelt gratitude
for their generous and steadfast support

Contents

Acknowledgments

Above all, we wish to thank the people who shared their stories with us. It was these individuals and their stories of healing and hope that inspired us to write this book. A number of others also helped us as we worked on this project. We are especially grateful to Dr. Bryan Gillespie, Emeritus Professor of English at Stetson University, who provided valuable editing suggestions. We also want to thank Rev. Jeffrey Sumner of Westminster-by-the-Sea Presbyterian Church and Rev. Paul Summer of All Saints Lutheran Church for their encouragement and advice. Finally, we want to express our appreciation to Michael West and Ann Delgehausen of Fortress Press, who shared our vision of helping churches reclaim their historical role as healing institutions.

Introduction

Why should religious congregations get actively involved in maintaining the health of their members and providing care to those in need? This is a question that each religious community and its leadership must ask. There are already so many demands on time and financial resources to support church organization and administration, youth programs, evangelism, missions, and more. Why would a congregation want to add another ministry—a health ministry—to its already packed list of responsibilities? Do churches really need to do this? Aren't there sufficient health care resources already available in most communities?

To answer these questions, we need to take a careful look at both our churches and our health care system. Mainline churches—Catholic, Lutheran, Methodist, Presbyterian, Episcopalian, and so on—have increasing numbers of older persons making up their congregations, and many of them have health problems. As of the year 2000, more than 50 percent of the members of mainline churches were over the age of sixty. Thus a large proportion of the membership is already at the age when significant health problems are more likely to occur. They will be relying more and more on the church in years ahead to meet their health care needs. Why is this so? Why the church?

Turning to the church for assistance with health care is nothing new. Throughout the past two thousand years, when people were elderly, sick, and too poor to afford their own health care, it was always religious organizations that provided for their needs. It was the church that built the first hospital for care of the sick in the general population in the fourth century. It was the church that built and staffed almost all hospitals in Western civilization over the next 1,400 years. It was the church that was responsible for the training of physicians for nearly a thousand years during the Middle Ages. The entire profession of nursing came directly out of the church, first with Catholic sisters (Sisters of Charity of St. Vincent de Paul) and then with Protestant deaconesses (trained by Lutherans in Germany). Even today, nearly one-third of American hospitals are in some way affiliated with a religious group. Furthermore, the primary source of volunteers who provide services for the sick in institutional and noninstitutional settings has been the church. In many ways, the church was the foremost provider of health care for centuries.

Wait a minute, you say. Most older adults today receive their health care from programs funded by the government or private health insurance. And most community hospitals, even those affiliated with a religious group, don't seem very interested in having local congregations involved in health care. At first glance it appears that there is no need for the church to expand its ministry to the sick beyond prayer and visitation. But a closer look reveals that dramatic demographic changes and immense economic pressures are creating a situation in which other institutions, particularly churches, will soon be called on to offer various forms of health care to their members and to the community at large.

It is no secret that the costs of health care are increasing every year. Medical advances and new drug treatments are wonderful, but very, very expensive. Health insurance premiums are rising. More and more people need health care every year. And our society is becoming less and less able to provide that health care. When Medicare began in the mid-1960s, its budget was less than $5 billion per year. By 1980 it had increased to $38 billion, and by 1992 it was more than $150 billion. Six years later it had grown to $230 billion per year, and, according to projections from the Department of Health and Human

Services, by 2007 the Medicare budget will exceed $415 billion per year.[1] Note that this increase in Medicare costs is occurring *before* the 75 million baby boomers enter their retirement years. Older boomers will reach retirement age by 2011. And by 2040, the number of persons over age sixty-five in the United States will have increased from around 35 million to nearly 80 million. With advances in medicine and increases in life expectancy, it is possible that the over-sixty-five population in the United States will exceed 100 million by that time. Despite new medical treatments for disease and disability, however, many of those 80 million to 100 million will have chronic health problems that require ongoing attention and care. These will include nearly 15 million with Alzheimer's disease and many millions more with crippling arthritis, stroke, diabetes, and chronic heart and lung diseases.

Where will all these older persons get their health care? After 2011, the government's ability to provide such services will become less and less. In fact, the entire health care system will be severely strained. According to Edward Schneider, dean of the Leonard Davis School of Gerontology and Andrus Gerontology Center at the University of Southern California, if research and medical advances continue at the current pace, life expectancy will continue to increase, but so will the period of time that people will be living with chronic diseases.[2] As community hospitals become like intensive care units, accepting only the sickest patients and rapidly discharging them to less intensive care settings, and nursing homes become like community hospitals, more and more responsibility for providing care for the chronically ill will reside with the patients' families. If the sick cannot afford twenty-four-hour nursing care in their homes, and if

---

1. S. Smith, M. Freedland, S. Heffler, D. McKusick, and The Health Expenditures Projection Team, "The Next Ten Years of Health Spending: What Does the Future Hold? *Health Affairs* 17 (1998): 128–40.

2. E. L. Schneider, "Aging in the Third Millennium. *Science* 283 (1999): 796–97.

they have no family, or family members are unable to care for them adequately, they will be forced to turn to the church for help. Then, churches will be forced into meeting the health needs of aging members—whether they are prepared to do so or not.

There is, however, an alternative course for churches. They don't have to wait until this tidal wave hits. They can begin right now to equip their members to address chronic diseases and other medical challenges. Already more and more responsibility for managing illnesses and health care is falling on the shoulders of patients and their families as people are discharged earlier and earlier from the acute care hospital and rehabilitation settings. Churches can help them with these responsibilities and burdens. Ministers, parish nurses, and concerned laypersons can provide patients and families with the information and support they need to manage these illnesses and to avoid complications and disability. They can arrange for life-saving medical services to be offered in congregational facilities, settings that are easily accessible and familiar to members of the church. Members can band together as teams to help individuals and families who have extraordinary illness-related burdens.

And it's not only the mainline churches with their largely older congregations that need to get involved in health ministries. The non-mainline churches, most with younger members, will eventually face similar problems. Fortunately, they are now in a position to help the members of their churches stay healthy so that they don't require as many health services later on. The costs of disease prevention programs are much less than the medical interventions necessary to treat diseases. It will also be important for churches to begin training younger members to provide support and care for elderly persons in the congregation, because it will be those young people who will be required to care for their elders at home and provide the volunteer services needed by churches in the future. Currently, children and young people have few role models in this regard. The multigeneration family is a rarity today, and many young persons grow up with little exposure to elderly persons. They do not understand the value of older adults or their possible contributions. It is crucial that churches wait no longer to train children to value and respect older members in their congregations and communities. Otherwise, in 2040, when those children are adults, they will be poorly prepared to provide the care their parents and grandparents will need. And the church will lack the volunteers necessary to provide those services that they will be called upon to offer.

But what will be the response of the medical community if churches decide to develop health ministries? Can faith communities and medical institutions work together?

Leaders in the health field are increasingly recognizing the valuable role churches and other religious institutions can play in health care. They see the many strengths and special resources churches can bring to a common mission of promoting health and preventing illness. They know that churches and other religious institutions are where we find large numbers of adults age fifty and over, and that it is persons in this age group who need education and support on health matters.

In addition to being "home" to large numbers of people who need this education and support, religious institutions have at least three important characteristics that enable them to play an important role in the health care arena. First, not only are they located throughout the community, but they are also generally established and governed in large measure by residents of the community. Therefore, they reflect the traditions and values of community residents and are generally trusted by them as well. Second, most religious congregations have well-established communication networks that allow them to stay in touch with members. Information about important medical matters and health care resources can be disseminated by announcements during congregational gatherings, bulletins distributed at worship services, mailings to members at their homes, e-mail messages, the church Web site, and volunteer phone networks. Third, and perhaps most important, religious institutions have strong traditions of volunteerism and civic engagement. In every congregation there are members who are willing not only to volunteer time, but also to participate in congregational training programs that enhance their ability to step into leadership roles and to be of service to others. By working closely with medical professionals, these individuals can organize programs that address many of the health needs of their congregations and the surrounding community.

Major medical centers, progressive health care systems, and charitable foundations are already taking steps to encourage religious congregations to increase their involvement in health care. Leaders of these organizations understand how people of faith, individually and collectively, can serve as valuable instruments of healing. For example, Duke University Medical Center has established a Center for the Study of Religion/Spirituality and Health. Faculty from the Division of Geriatric Medicine and Gerontology at the Johns Hopkins University School of Medicine have worked closely with community hospitals and religious congregations to develop lay health education and patient advocacy programs. Several major hospital systems in Florida, a state already experiencing the demographic changes that will eventually sweep the rest of the country, have developed alliances with many congregations. The Robert Wood Johnson Foundation, the nation's largest foundation devoted to improving the health and health care of Americans, has pledged $100 million to fund a nationwide Faith in Action Program. Over the next seven years, this program will provide grants to two thousand coalitions of religious congregations that bring together volunteers to offer care for the chronically ill and disabled. The John Templeton Foundation is providing financial support for medical school courses to train doctors about the importance of religion in maintaining health and the value of networking with local congregations and pastors (nearly eighty of the 126 medical schools in the United States now have such courses).

What about the members of churches? How do they feel about congregational health ministries? Do they really want health programs offered in their churches?

We have found that among churchgoers there is already an awareness of the need for their congregations to offer health programs. In a recent survey of more than five hundred people representing a religiously diverse group of churches, 85 percent said they wanted health programs held at their church. They wanted programs on stress management, Alzheimer's disease, cancer, heart disease, depression, cardiopulmonary resuscitation (CPR), living wills, arthritis, and a number of other health issues. Eighty percent reported that they believed there was a need for their church to sponsor support groups, and a similar percentage wanted their church to sponsor exercise programs. Seventy-five percent wanted health screenings (blood pressure, cholesterol, and diabetes, for example) and preventive interventions (such as flu vaccinations) to be available at church. And interestingly, 45 percent of those surveyed indicated they would be willing to volunteer their time to help organize or promote these programs.

Clearly, the need exists to strengthen our ways of providing health care. Just as clearly, ordinary laypersons are aware of this need, and many are ready and willing to volunteer. This book attempts to show one way of providing that needed strength by mobilizing volunteers through communities of faith—neighborhood churches.

In the chapters that follow we report on the experiences of a number of churches that have already recognized and responded to the health concerns of their members and, in many cases, the community at large. Ministers, parish nurses, and laypersons, dedicated to extending the healing ministry of Jesus through congregational health ministries, have found creative ways to work in partnership with health care institutions and professionals.

The chapters are case studies in how insight and commitment can be combined with knowledge and organization to produce ministry. The stories told here do not produce a strict formula to be followed by any church that wants to launch a health ministry. Instead, they show some of the many ways in which communities of faith have responded to the need. In recounting these experiences, we hope to inspire and encourage churches and other individual members of religious congregations to act on the impulses of their caring hearts and, in turn, reap the rewards that invariably come to those who give of themselves for the good of others. We begin with the story of how one woman's desire to help, with the encouragement of an insightful pastor, transformed the attitude of an entire congregation about the importance of a healthful lifestyle and in all probability saved the lives of more than one member, as well as prevented the development of serious complications from unsuspected diseases in others, the pastor included.

chapter one

An Instrument of Healing

If you were to meet Nancy Force, it would probably
never occur to you that she is a modern-day healer—someone who
has been responsible for restoring people to health and saving individuals from serious medical conditions that can cripple and kill. You
wouldn't see any of the outward signs we typically associate with
medicine and health care in the twenty-first century. She doesn't wear
a white coat. She doesn't have a stethoscope around her neck. And she
doesn't work in any capacity at the local hospital. Instead, you probably would guess that Nancy is retired and a grandmother. And you
would be right on both counts. She retired from a successful career in
the business world a number of years ago, and she is not only a
grandmother but a great-grandmother as well, with sixteen grand-
children and two great-grandchildren.

What you would notice and remember about Nancy would be her
warmth and sincere interest in others—the way she reaches out to
people and literally touches them. Sometimes it is with a hug, even if
it is her first time meeting them. Other times it may be a handshake
that lasts a little longer than most and somehow conveys a genuine
sense of concern. If you had been next to her at a meal, you probably
would recall how she gently but firmly held your hand as she gave
thanks for both the food and the opportunity to be together. You also
probably would remember her words as you parted, a simple yet
heartfelt "God bless" or "God be with you."

If you ask people who have worked with Nancy to describe her, you'll find that they all start with the same word—enthusiastic! When Nancy has an idea about something that she thinks is worth trying, her face lights up and she gets so excited that she may have trouble sitting or standing still as she talks about it. If it's an idea for something she and her church should try, you can be sure that she'll be rubbing her arms and legs as she describes it. This is her reaction to the "goose bumps" that have come over her. For Nancy, they are a sure sign that the idea she has is not her own but from the Holy Spirit. They also signal important work for her to do.

So, if Nancy is retired and has never attended medical or nursing school, how can she be considered a healer? How can someone with no formal training in medicine have the ability to save lives and restore people to health? Can she really do any more than pray for the sick and offer comforting words and touch when they are in the hospital or ill at home?

One person who has no doubts about Nancy's abilities as a healer is Rev. Jeffrey Sumner, the senior pastor at Westminster-by-the-Sea Presbyterian Church in Daytona Beach, Florida. If asked about Nancy, he will enthusiastically testify to the impact of her health-related church work, citing as evidence several members of the congregation who have been saved from life-threatening diseases and crippling conditions. In fact, he is one of them. He had no way of knowing, of course, that he would reap such a significant personal reward when he was contacted by Halifax Medical Center, a nearby community hospital, and asked if any members of his congregation might be interested in a new program to train volunteers from churches and synagogues as lay health educators.

The Lay Health Education program had its origins at nearby Stetson University, where I (WDH) taught and served as the director of the Center for the Study of Aging and Health. Dwaine Cochran, one of my colleagues in the Department of Psychology, and I had become concerned about many of the changes in the health care system. Economic pressures were forcing hospitals to discharge patients after shorter and shorter stays, leaving patients and their families with greater responsibility for managing health matters. But few people were prepared for this. They needed more medical information and resources, and they needed them close to home. Physicians and their staff, operating under increasing pressures from managed care companies to see more and more patients, had little time to educate and prepare patients and families to manage their health conditions when they left the hospital or the doctor's office. And if they had questions or something went wrong, it was increasingly difficult to find someone who knew enough to guide them. We believed this critical gap in the average person's health care system needed to be bridged.

Working with faculty from the Division of Geriatric Medicine and Gerontology at the Johns Hopkins University School of Medicine, we developed a program to train volunteers from religious congregations to serve as lay health educators. This training would give volunteers the tools they needed to coordinate health education seminars, screenings, and support groups in their congregations. One of the distinctive elements of the program was that the volunteers did not need to have any particular background or prior training. All that was required was a genuine interest in learning more about how to help people maintain their health and to manage illnesses effectively when they did occur. Physicians and other health professionals associated with the hospital would provide the training and ongoing support these lay leaders would need.

Rev. Sumner saw at once that this program would appeal to someone like Nancy Force, whose caring spirit was obvious to those who knew her. It would play to her strengths. Rev. Sumner had often described her role within the congregation as that of a Barnabas (an encourager and enabler) or an Andrew (a connector). He also knew that her own experiences of caring for her late husband during the chemotherapy and multiple surgeries he endured as he battled cancer had left her full of compassion and eager to find new ways to reach out to people in need. And he knew that she could pull together the people and resources that would be necessary to make the program a success.

When Nancy heard about this program, she realized that it was exactly what she had been looking for. There were so many times she had said, "I want to know *how* to help people! I want to learn what to *do!*" Plus, as Nancy thought about this opportunity, she got a major case of those goose bumps. There could be no doubt in her mind—this was something she was being called to do.

For eight weeks Nancy and fifteen other volunteers from various congregations met at the hospital for two hours each Thursday afternoon. Here physicians and other health professionals shared with them valuable information about potentially life-threatening and life-limiting conditions. They learned about the dangers and burdens of cancer, heart disease, depression, diabetes, hypertension, and Alzheimer's disease. More important, they learned about ways that they could help people prevent or gain control over such diseases. Through the classes they discovered that they could do more than offer prayers and words of comfort. Armed with the knowledge and resources the physicians and hospital staff were offering, they now could actually change the course of these potentially devastating diseases. They now had the tools to heal.

The church volunteers also heard physicians and health professionals humbly acknowledge their own limitations. In spite of years of training and ready access to the latest developments in medical science, they were often powerless. But they saw that the Lay Health Education Program would provide a new way to reach so many of the people who needed medical care—people who might lose their life because cancer was not detected early enough to be successfully treated, individuals who might lose a leg or their eyesight because diabetes was never diagnosed, those who might have a stroke or heart attack because they were not treated for hypertension, those who might never enjoy life or who might even decide that life is no longer worth living because of untreated depression. Overextended doctors and nurses and other medical professionals recognized that the work of preventing disease and restoring people to health could no longer be reserved solely for professionals operating within the confines of a medical institution. They saw the need for people like Nancy to become their partners in healing. Working together, they could share life-saving information and resources with the people who needed them the most.

Nancy immediately took the tools she had been given in the Lay Health Education Program and began building a new model of ministry. Working closely with her pastors and members of her congregation and frequently with members of nearby congregations, she developed a series of programs that educated and empowered. In the familiar and secure setting of their church, people were able to obtain the information and many of the services they needed to maintain or restore their own health or that of loved ones.

Nancy's fellow members at Westminster-by-the-Sea Presbyterian Church enthusiastically embraced these programs, as did Rev. Sumner, their pastor. It was clear that the health programs met an important need. People from the church and the community wanted to hear reliable information about the various steps they could take to prevent, or at least control, serious chronic conditions such as hypertension, heart disease, and diabetes. They wanted to know more about cancer and the importance of early detection. They were eager to learn how to recognize and respond to depression, and how to ease the burden of those who care for family members with Alzheimer's disease and other incurable, progressive illnesses.

Spurred to action by the growing interest in these health programs, the church's Outreach Committee adopted them as part of their mission, and Nancy and her fellow committee members found more ways to minister to the health needs of the people. These included arranging for flu vaccinations and screenings for hypertension, diabetes, skin cancer, and high cholesterol at the church—all things that could be arranged by an individual, but very few did so, and then often only after symptoms had suggested the need for a particular test.

From the beginning, Rev. Sumner recognized the value of this work and viewed it as an important ministry that enabled the church to reclaim its theological and historical mission of healing the sick. But as much as he appreciated and supported the health programs,

Rev. Sumner had no thought that he might someday benefit directly. He was in his early forties and feeling good about his life and his work. His health seemed to be fine, although he had put on a few pounds over the years—something he attributed to careless eating habits and not enough exercise. The only physical or mental changes he had noticed seemed minor, and a couple of the changes even seemed positive—he had lost a little weight recently, and he was drinking a lot more water. Of somewhat greater concern was the fact that he seemed more "scatterbrained" and had to rely more on his notes while delivering sermons. (He was also more forgetful around the house, and his teenage children loved to kid him about the time they discovered he had absentmindedly put the peanut butter in the freezer.) But overall, there seemed little reason for him to worry about his health.

Reason for concern appeared, however, in June of 1999 when he attended a health program sponsored by the Outreach Committee at Westminster-by-the-Sea. This program, part of a series titled "Our Body, Mind, and Soul," focused on diabetes. As pastor, Rev. Sumner was there primarily to show support for the work of Nancy Force and the others on the Outreach Committee. When more people than expected showed up and it looked as if there would not be enough resources to handle everyone, he volunteered to forgo the screenings himself. Fortunately, additional materials were found and he was able to participate along with the others. To his great surprise, the test showed that his blood sugar was abnormally high. Concerned that this might be a mistake, they tested him again. The numbers came out the same—a blood sugar of more than 300. Rev. Sumner knew what this meant. Through the programs offered at his church, he had learned that diabetes was a serious medical condition that, if ignored, could have dire consequences. He realized that he needed to get help for his diabetes, but he was not certain exactly where to turn or what to do.

Rev. Sumner did not have to wait to get answers to the questions that were running through his head. The health professionals conducting the screenings that day had the answers. They told him about a diabetes program offered by the hospital and encouraged him to sign up for it. He decided to enroll at once, and he was glad he did. Although it was disturbing to learn about the potentially devastating consequences of diabetes—the increased risk of amputations, blindness, kidney disease, stroke, and heart attack—it was reassuring to learn that there were measures he could take to control it.

As important as it was for Rev. Sumner to discover that he had diabetes and to learn what to do to bring it under control, it was implementing these changes that presented the greatest challenge. Simply remembering to take medication every day would not be enough. He was going to have to make significant, lasting changes in his daily routines. Some deeply ingrained habits were going to have to go. One of the biggest changes was in his diet and eating habits. (His first thought: "Oh no! No more Krispy Kreme doughnuts or brownies!") Making changes in eating habits is hard for anyone, but it presents a special challenge for individuals like Rev. Sumner who have to eat away from home so often. Indeed, they are at the mercy of those who invite them to their homes for dinner or prepare church meals.

Always eating the right foods to control his diabetes could have been extremely difficult, perhaps impossible, if Rev. Sumner had been forced to take it on solely by himself. But he didn't have to bear all the responsibility. When members of the church learned about his diabetes, they stepped forward to help. Because of the work of Nancy and the others who had offered health programs, church members knew that it was often the support and cooperation of family and friends that made the critical difference in the successful treatment of conditions like diabetes. They realized that they could play a vital role in helping their pastor and others with diabetes remain faithful to their special diet by making sure that every church dinner included appropriate food choices. Parishioners who invited Rev. Sumner and his wife for dinner made similar provisions. Congregation members realized that they had an opportunity to participate in this all-important dimension of healing. In fact, at this point they were in a much better position than the doctors and nurses to have a positive effect on the health of their pastor and others in the congregation who had diabetes.

But diabetes wasn't the only disease that took on special meaning for Rev. Sumner and the parishioners at Westminster-by-the-Sea Presbyterian, a church located only a few hundred yards from a beach well known for "fun in the sun." Recent events had made them painfully aware of the grave dangers of skin cancer. Within a period of less than eighteen months they lost two members of their church family, both men in their thirties, to melanoma, the deadliest form of skin cancer. Having seen the dreadful effects of the disease on these men and their families, a number of church members felt called to take steps to prevent it from happening again. They knew they must do something to help other individuals and families avoid the suffering and loss that accompany this deadly cancer.

Now acutely conscious of the importance of early detection and treatment, they first strongly urged all members to have regular screenings for skin cancer. But they did more than this. Realizing that some people might find it difficult to get to a doctor or clinic to be checked, they made arrangements for screenings to be done at the church. It took only a few months for church members to see compelling evidence of the value of these screenings: Three members of the congregation were found to have suspicious moles or growths that required medical attention. And then there was one member, a vibrant woman in her forties, who discovered that she had more than suspicious moles or growths. She had melanoma, the same disease that had killed the two young men. But the outcome for her would be entirely different. Because the melanoma was detected in its earliest stage, she was treated and cured. For her, the skin cancer screening was a life-saving experience.

Still another step taken by many members of the congregation was to support the work of the parents of one of the young men who had died from melanoma. Bill and Pat Walter were determined that out of their pain and loss would come something that could help others: They decided to establish a charitable foundation. Their purpose was twofold—to provide aid to families who had a loved one with melanoma and to support research on this deadly cancer. The church continues not only to make a sizable contribution to the foundation

each year, but also to help the parents with an annual walk that is designed to raise both awareness and funds. In fact, Rev. Sumner and
many members of Westminster-by-the-Sea take part in the walk and
solicit financial support for their participation from friends and busi-
nesses in the community.

These personal stories are just a few examples of how important
health ministries have become to the life and mission of Westminster-
by-the-Sea Presbyterian Church. A program that started with Nancy
Force's desire to learn how to help people has evolved into one that
offers regular screenings for skin cancer, cholesterol, and diabetes; flu
vaccinations every fall; a walking club for those who need to increase
their physical activity; and even CPR training. People who want to
learn more about depression, living wills, hospice care, medication
interactions, or how to support families caring for a loved one with
Alzheimer's disease can attend classes and discussion groups at the
church. In addition, the church's commitment to health ministries
has made it possible for individuals and families touched by alcoholism to find support from Alcoholics Anonymous and Al-Anon
groups that meet regularly at the church.

Rev. Sumner speaks with passion and conviction about his
church's commitment to become a healing institution. "Our congregation's involvement in health ministries has created a new dimension in our care for one another as we share common weaknesses and
possible solutions. We find ourselves more in tune with each other
and more in tune with God's vision for us as a church because of our
involvement in this health ministry."

Koenig's Corner

Because of the strong association between being overweight and being
a church member (demonstrated by scientific research over and over
again), and the strong correlation between being overweight and having diabetes, the church is a natural place to screen for this devastating
medical condition. If diabetes is caught early on, weight control and
diet can help forestall many of the secondary complications, including

loss of vision, kidney problems, chronic pain from diabetic neuropathy, amputation because of poor circulation, stroke, and heart attack, to mention just a few. Given the increasing barriers to the receipt of good preventive medical care (especially the lack of health insurance), it becomes especially important for the church to begin cooperating with health institutions to make health education and disease screening easier. The church is the only place in society where people of all ages congregate on a regular basis, and it is therefore an ideal place to screen for treatable health problems. Because the body is the temple of the soul and is necessary to carry out the ministries that many of us have been called to, attention to health issues becomes almost as important to the church as maintaining the spiritual lives of the membership. We are not simply made up of bodies, minds, and spirit—we are all three at once. Anything that affects the body will affect the spirit, and anything that affects the spirit will affect the mind, and so on. Producing whole and functioning humans—ready and able to love our God and love our neighbor—is part of the mission of the church, and that wholeness includes the physical and emotional dimensions.

Diabetes—Some Basic Information

- Approximately 17 million Americans (6 percent of the population) have diabetes.
- Almost 6 million of these people have not yet been diagnosed.
- Approximately 20 percent of adults age sixty-five and over have diabetes.
- Type II diabetes (previously called non-insulin-dependent diabetes mellitus) accounts for 90 to 95 percent of the diagnosed cases of diabetes.
- Diabetes is the seventh leading cause of death in the United States.

- People with diabetes are at an increased risk of heart disease, stroke, blindness, kidney disease, and amputations.
- Diabetes is the number one cause of new cases of blindness in adults ages twenty to seventy-four.
- Diabetes is the number one cause of end-stage renal disease.

What Can Be Done in Your Congregation

- Distribute information about the prevalence of diabetes. This will help people see that it is a condition that is likely to affect a significant number of individuals in the congregation. Encourage members to share this information with family and friends who are not a part of the congregation.
- When distributing information on diabetes, make a special effort to target groups that are at greater risk—older adults, for instance. In the sixty-five-and-over age group, as many as one in five is likely to have diabetes.
- Impress upon people the potentially severe consequences of untreated diabetes. The absence of symptoms does not necessarily mean that no damage is being done to their body.
- Offer hope! With good medical care and self-management, diabetes can be controlled and its health consequences greatly limited.
- Arrange with a hospital or medical laboratory to provide screenings at a time and location convenient for most members—after religious services at the church, for example.
- Educate the entire congregation on the dietary needs of people with diabetes, and be certain to offer appropriate food choices at all church meals.
- Find ways to encourage and support regular exercise and weight control. One approach is to have a walking group that meets regularly at the church.
- Offer emotional support to individuals and families. They shouldn't have to go through this alone.

Skin Cancer—Some Basic Information

- More than 50,000 new cases of melanoma are reported to the American Cancer Society each year; in the past ten years, new cases of melanoma have been increasing more rapidly than any other type of cancer.
- More than 800,000 new cases of basal-cell skin cancer are reported each year.
- More than 200,000 new cases of squamous-cell skin cancer are reported each year.
- Almost 10,000 people die of skin cancer each year.
- The main cause of skin cancer is exposure to the sun.
- If all skin cancers were detected early enough, the cure rate would be nearly 100 percent.

What Can Be Done in Your Congregation

- Distribute information about the prevalence and dangers of skin cancer.
- Target the groups most likely to spend much of their time in the sun.
- Provide members with instructions about how to do self-examinations and what to look for.
- Provide information about the steps they can take to prevent skin cancer
    - avoid sun exposure between 10 A.M. and 2 P.M.
    - use lotions with an SPF of 15 or higher
    - wear hats and protective clothing
- Arrange for screenings to be offered at church.

chapter two

The Good Shepherd's Hope

It was during a long walk on one of his favorite beaches that Rev. Bill Barnes, pastor of St. Luke's United Methodist Church in Orlando, Florida, experienced the strong, unmistakable awareness of God's presence and the call to lead a new ministry—a ministry of health and healing. He was to find a way to deliver health care to the thousands of men, women, and children in his community who were not receiving adequate medical care because they lacked health insurance.

Rev. Barnes was surprised by his new calling. It was overwhelming to even think about how this could be accomplished, and there was nothing in his training or background to prepare him for such an assignment. Nevertheless, he knew that it was an important mission, and one that he must take on.

The first day back from vacation, Rev. Barnes prayed for guidance and assistance. Certain that he had been called to establish a health center, but also well aware that he did not have the knowledge and skills to do it by himself, he prayed that he would find two people who could help him get started. He felt that he needed both a medical doctor and a "big picture" person to work with him on this project.

That same morning, not too long after praying for help, a member of the congregation, Kathy Mansfield, stepped into his office and told him that she was there to talk to him about finding a church-related project that her husband, Todd, an executive with the Disney organization, could participate in—one that would use his talents. Rev. Barnes, familiar with this man's experience supervising major projects from conception to full operation, realized that he had just found his "big picture" person.

Two hours later, Brenda Deaver, another member of the congregation, came by the church to talk with Rev. Barnes. She too was there to discuss the need to find a church-related project for her husband, Mike, a physician. At this point, Rev. Barnes knew his prayers had been answered. Before noon on his first day back from vacation, the same vacation during which he had heard the call to start a health clinic, Rev. Barnes had already found the two people he would need to help him carry out the new vision.

Rev. Barnes's next step was to set up a meeting with both of these men. The following morning the three of them met at Sand Lake Hospital, where Mike had to make early morning rounds. Sitting at a table in the hospital cafeteria, Mike and Todd listened to Rev. Barnes tell the story of his call to meet the health needs of people without health insurance or any other means of obtaining medical care. He admitted that he didn't know where they should start or what form the center would eventually take, but he was certain that he was to establish the clinic and that now was the time to begin the work.

After some initial discussion about the many challenges they would face, including significant legal and financial obstacles, they decided to bring some more people onto their team. Knowing that twelve was a good number for initiating a ministry, they came up with the names of nine more members of the congregation who could help.

The first challenge this twelve-person team realized they would have to confront was the concern among physicians and other health care professionals about the possibility of malpractice suits. They felt that many health professionals would want to volunteer their services for a faith-based health clinic but would be reluctant to do so if it meant they risked being sued. Fortunately, the team discovered that the Florida legislature had enacted a health care providers statute that granted immunity from malpractice suits to health professionals who offer their services for free to individuals whose incomes are no greater than 150 percent of the federal poverty level and who have no health insurance. As long as the clinic worked with this group of people, which was exactly the group Rev. Barnes had felt called to serve, the health care providers would not have to worry about lawsuits.

The next challenge the team addressed was finding a location for the clinic. They wanted a site near the community they would be serving, and one that individuals of any ethnic group or faith would feel comfortable visiting. As they researched potential sites, they learned that a number of public schools in the county had been given special funding to build family health centers, but that they were sitting unused because no money had been provided to staff the clinics. One of these health centers was located at a school in the area they would be serving. Working through a church member who was an administrator in the public school system, they were able to obtain permission to use the clinic at this school as well as the other seven schools.

Finding equipment for the clinic was the next task they faced. Here again, it was a member of the congregation who came to their aid. This member worked at the warehouse of Florida Hospital and was able to arrange for the hospital to donate the equipment that would be needed at the clinic.

The next challenge was to arrange for the medical tests the doctors would want to order. This was accomplished when Health Central Hospital in Ocoee, Florida, whose president, Richard Irwin, was a member of the team of twelve, offered to donate radiology and laboratory services.

They would also need prescription medications for many of the patients they would be seeing. This potential obstacle was largely overcome when they found that they could obtain much of what they would need through donations from physicians and pharmaceutical companies. As for the medications that they could not get donated, a pharmacy agreed to sell these to patients at reduced prices.

The next step was to choose a name for the center, a name that would reflect both its mission and the motivation of the people who organized and would operate the center. Rev. Barnes recommended that they call it Shepherd's Hope. He suggested this name because it was the hope of Jesus, the Good Shepherd, that we would take care of each other. It now looked as if the essential components of a health clinic were coming together. This meant the volunteers were at a point where they would need some legal assistance to formalize some of these arrangements. Before Rev. Barnes could contact any attorneys he knew, a letter from an attorney arrived at his office. In this letter the attorney explained that she and other attorneys in her office had experience in health law and wanted to volunteer their services to the health clinic that they had heard Rev. Barnes and members of his congregation were organizing.

With key pieces of the puzzle in place, Rev. Barnes felt it was time to tell the entire congregation about his call to establish a health center for the working poor and about the developments that had ensued. At a Sunday worship service in December he shared his story. At the conclusion of the story, he asked members who wanted to be part of a miracle to come to the church on Tuesday night.

When Rev. Barnes walked into the church Tuesday evening, he found more than 200 members of the congregation waiting for him. He explained that rather than simply giving them an outline of the plans for a clinic and then passing around a sign-up sheet asking for volunteers, he wanted *them* to spend the next hour designing the clinic. He told them, "We're going to make a clinic, and we're going to do it tonight."

They then split into groups. Physicians, nurses, and other health professionals met as one group. Those with experience in medical records made up a second group. Others were formed around the topics of supplies acquisition, administrative processes, marketing and advertising, and the general responsibilities of volunteers. Each group was instructed to organize their part of the clinic. Rev. Barnes moved among the groups as they outlined both the needs and the opportunities in their respective areas. By the end of the evening, a comprehensive plan for the volunteer health clinic had emerged. Rev. Barnes now felt confident that the clinic could be in operation within a few months.

A key aspect of the clinic was that there would be a role for virtually everyone who wanted to be a part of this ministry of health and healing. Shepherd's Hope needed more than doctors, nurses, and physicians' assistants. The clinic needed people with expertise in advertising and public relations to get the word out to the community. It also needed greeters and receptionists to welcome patients coming to the clinic. Other volunteers were needed to conduct eligibility interviews and to assist with pharmacy work and record keeping. And, of course, there was a need for someone to step in as executive director. As had happened with every other challenge they had faced, the right person appeared at the right time. In this case, it was Dr. Ruth McKeefery, a retired university professor and administrator, who offered to serve as executive director on a volunteer basis.

It was now February 1997—less than six months since Rev. Barnes had received his call to start a health clinic and only two months since sharing the story with the congregation of St. Luke's United Methodist Church—and Shepherd's Hope was ready to open.

Dr. Christopher Crotty, a dermatologist, and Dr. Bonnie Dean, an internist, were on duty the first evening the clinic opened its doors. The first patient to enter was an unemployed nurse who felt she was in good health but needed to have a physical examination in order to apply for a position in the medical field. Being unemployed, she had no health insurance to cover the cost of an appointment with a physician. Dr. Dean was glad to help by giving her a thorough examination, one that the patient later described as the best physical examination she had ever received. At the conclusion of the exam, Dr. Dean suggested that she also have a Pap smear taken. The patient initially declined the offer, but eventually she was persuaded that it would be a good idea—and it was. The results revealed that she had stage three cervical cancer, a condition that required immediate treatment.

The doctors and staff at Shepherd's Hope were able to arrange for surgery and postoperative care for this woman. Thankfully, the surgery was successful. The cancer had been caught in time. Within a few weeks the woman was able to return to work as a nurse, and she also returned to Shepherd's Hope, but this time as a volunteer instead of as a patient.

The nurse with cervical cancer wasn't the only patient that first night. In fact, Dr. Crotty, who had thought that there might be no use for his special expertise, found that the next three patients all had skin conditions.

These types of "miracle coincidences" have continued throughout the six years that Shepherd's Hope has been in operation. A good example is the Spanish-speaking psychiatrist who got his dates confused and showed up on an evening when he wasn't scheduled to work. He was urged to stay, though, just in case he might be needed. It turned out to be quite fortunate that he did, because one of the patients who came to the clinic that evening was a Hispanic woman suffering from bipolar (manic-depressive) disorder, a serious condition that required the special care of a psychiatrist.

The demand for a wide range of medical services grew as word of the clinic spread throughout the community. Soon Shepherd's Hope needed to expand its hours. It began opening its doors a second evening every week.

The model of health ministry that had emerged from the work of Rev. Barnes and members of the congregation at St. Luke's United Methodist Church was clearly a success, not only for the thousands of people who were being cared for, but also for the hundreds of people who were giving of their time and talents to provide the care. This community of faith had succeeded in bringing together caring people, both medical professionals and laypersons, and people who needed care.

Other churches in central Florida learned of the work of Shepherd's Hope and were inspired to establish similar programs in their communities. The Seventh-Day Adventist church adjacent to the main campus of Florida Hospital, the flagship institution of the Adventist Health System, decided to partner with the hospital and establish a volunteer health clinic at a high school. Northland Community Church, an interdenominational Christian church, was next, followed by First Presbyterian Church of Orlando, St. John Vianney Catholic

Church, Macedonia Missionary Baptist Church, and, most recently, St. Luke's Lutheran Church.

One reason these ministries spread around the central Florida community was the influence of Shepherd's Hope volunteers, many of whom had come from churches that were not a part of the Shepherd's Hope network. The health center sponsored by St. Luke's Lutheran Church in Oviedo, for example, traces its beginning to a nurse from the congregation who had volunteered at one of the Shepherd's Hope clinics. She was so impressed by what she saw that she spoke to one of her pastors, Rev. Brian Roberts, about their church becoming affiliated with Shepherd's Hope and starting a health clinic in their community. Rev. Roberts was quite receptive to this suggestion. Having served as a volunteer firefighter and emergency medical technician in his previous pastorate, Rev. Roberts knew firsthand the valuable contributions that volunteers could make as well as the rewards that come from helping others in need.

As Rev. Roberts and a few members of St. Luke's Lutheran Church began to explore what would be involved in establishing a health clinic, there was a development within the congregation that strengthened their motivation to mount the project. Shortly after a member of the congregation died of a heart attack, Rev. Roberts learned from the man's family that he had been experiencing some of the warning signs of serious heart disease for two weeks prior to his heart attack but had not seen a doctor because he did not have health insurance. Rev. Roberts realized that there was a good chance the fatal heart attack could have been prevented if there had been a Shepherd's Hope clinic in their community. Clearly, St. Luke's needed to move ahead.

Rev. Roberts's subsequent discussions with Cindi Kopelman, the executive director of Shepherd's Hope, were encouraging. It appeared that St. Luke's Lutheran Church had the resources to establish a Shepherd's Hope clinic. The church would, however, have to overcome a hurdle the other churches had not faced. Unlike all the other churches that made up Shepherd's Hope, St. Luke's was located in Seminole County, not Orange County. Since Seminole County schools did not have any medical clinics, the church would have to find another facility. Fortunately, there were a number of unused rooms available in the building that had until recently served as the church's school. With some renovations, these rooms could serve as the clinic.

Rev. Roberts took the idea for a Shepherd's Hope clinic to the church's board of directors and then on to the full congregation. After winning the strong endorsement of both of these groups, Rev. Roberts and his committee were ready to recruit volunteers. They immediately had sixty members offering help. Interestingly, the fact that there were only two physicians in the congregation did not prove to be a problem. Several members of the congregation recruited their own personal physicians for the program. They were joined by other physicians and health care professionals in the community who were not members of St. Luke's Lutheran Church but had heard about the program.

Members of the congregation who did not have any training or experience in the medical field but wanted to be a part of this new ministry found many ways they could help. While some volunteered to be trained as eligibility interviewers or pharmacy assistants, others assisted with obtaining medical supplies or publicizing the clinic by sending flyers to schools and churches and writing press releases for the media outlets. Other members donated furnishings that helped give the clinic an inviting and comfortable atmosphere. By December 2002, the clinic at St. Luke's Lutheran Church, the seventh health center in the Shepherd's Hope network, was ready to open its doors.

The accomplishments of this faith-based organization are truly extraordinary. In the six years that Shepherd's Hope has been in operation, it has provided more than 20,000 patient visits to men, women, and children. In 2002 alone there were almost 8,000 patient visits, and currently there are more than 800 volunteers actively involved in its work. Shepherd's Hope demonstrates the powerful healing potential that resides in our churches, a potential that can be realized when people who are committed to caring for those in need embrace a creative vision of ministry.

Koenig's Corner

There is a large and growing number of people in the United States who are uninsured. Health care costs and health insurance premiums continue to rise, and the problem only worsens in times of economic downturn. In spite of total health care spending of $1.3 trillion in the United States in the year 2000 (all sources, government and citizens, public and private health care), approximately 39 million Americans were uninsured. Even using a very conservative rate-increase estimate of 6 percent per year, economists have predicted that total health care spending (all sources) could easily exceed $1.7 trillion by 2007. In fact, 2001's 6 percent figure was already surpassed by 2.7 percent: Health care spending that year rose to $1.4 trillion and accounted for 14.1 percent of the total economy ("Spending on Health Care Increased Sharply in 2001," *New York Times*, January 8, 2003). It's the largest increase on record. That same year, the number of uninsured increased from 39 million to 41 million, despite government efforts to stem this trend (Table HI-2 "Health Insurance Coverage Status and Type of Coverage—All People by Age and Sex: 1987 to 2001" U.S. Census Bureau, 2002).

Faith-based efforts such as those exemplified by Shepherd's Hope are desperately needed in uncertain economic times and will only be needed more as health care costs rise and public resources to support such care dwindle. People who are served by such clinics experience firsthand that the church in America is not irrelevant or superfluous, but that it can indeed make a vital difference during a time of need.

chapter three

Finding a Life Line

One of the most familiar faces around Trinity
Lutheran Church in Kissimmee, Florida, is that of Vince Grande. You
will find him there almost every day of the week, even though he is
not a member of the church staff. A retired U.S. Army officer (and
West Point graduate) whose assignments took him to Germany, Viet-
nam, Hawaii, and Washington, D.C., Vince now spends most of his
time volunteering in several different capacities at the church. On
weekdays he serves as an assistant to the computer lab teacher at the
church's school, where he shares with students as young as three some
of the knowledge he gained working with computers for more than
forty years. Although he enjoys helping students with all aspects of
computing, his favorite time is when he gets to teach them about
computer hardware. He loves to dismantle a computer to show students the various parts and demonstrate how they work. Students say
that this is also their favorite part of the class. They enjoy seeing
floppy drives, hard drives, and CD drives opened up, and they love
having the opportunity to play with them. They think "Mr. Vince" is
cool to let them do this.

It's not just during the day that you will find Vince at Trinity. He
often returns in the evening. On Wednesdays he's there for the
church dinner and choir practice, and on the last Monday of each
month he is back in the evening to attend the meeting of the church
council.

On Sundays you can find Vince in the choir—he is pretty easy to spot in the bass section with his short military-style haircut. On some Sundays he not only sings in the choir, but also serves as lector, coming down from the choir loft to the altar to read the first and second Scripture lessons of the day. But there is one Sunday each year, usually in early fall, when individuals attending a worship service at Trinity have an opportunity to hear Vince do more than sing or read Scripture. It is on this Sunday that he is called on to make a special announcement about a health program the church offers. As he speaks to the congregation, Vince does more than simply describe the program and inform parishioners when and where it will be held. He gives a passionate appeal for them to participate, because it could save their lives. He speaks with such conviction because, as he explains, the program did save his life. He tells them, "I would not be here today had it not been for this particular health ministry program offered at the church." And then he shares his story.

In August of 1999, he had scheduled an appointment with his family physician. He made this appointment not because he was experiencing pain or any distressing symptoms, but because he knew that he needed help kicking his smoking habit. In spite of feeling that he was in good health, he was aware that smoking posed a serious threat to his physical well-being and that he needed to stop. But he also knew that the addictive properties of cigarettes made it almost impossible to stop if he didn't have some medication to help him. During the appointment, Vince's physician conducted a routine physical examination. He listened with his stethoscope to Vince's chest, neck, and the calves of his legs. Vince noticed that he spent more time than usual checking the carotid arteries in his neck. After listening carefully, the doctor told Vince that he had heard a bruit, or swishing sound, that could indicate a blockage. Since such a blockage can be life threatening and often requires surgery, he recommended that Vince obtain a carotid scan at a nearby outpatient clinic. He also wanted a scan of Vince's legs to check peripheral blood flow.

Two weeks later Vince had the scans done. After a few days, he concluded that the tests must not have revealed any problems, because the technician who conducted the scans had said nothing and his doctor had not called him to discuss the results. Relieved, Vince went about his various activities at home and church without thinking much more about his health.

It was almost a month later that Vince decided to accompany his wife, Gloria, to a health screening that was being held at their church. The newly formed health ministry team, working closely with Pastor Peter Zieg, had arranged for an organization called Life Line to bring its mobile unit to the church to offer three tests that could detect potentially serious medical problems. One of these was a scan of the carotid arteries, similar to the test Vince had had a few weeks earlier. The second screened for the existence of an aneurysm in the abdominal artery, and the third for peripheral arterial disease (plaque buildup). Once Gloria and Vince arrived, he decided that given the convenience and relatively inexpensive cost of the tests, he would also have them done. What harm could there be in having a second set of tests?

A few weeks later Vince was surprised when he received his Life Line results via special delivery. The leg scan (for peripheral arterial disease) revealed no problems, but the other tests indicated he had blockage in his right carotid artery and an abdominal aneurysm. Life Line recommended that he see his doctor immediately. Vince's doctor was quite surprised and concerned when he saw the results. Vince's earlier carotid scan at the outpatient clinic had indicated there was no more than 50 percent blockage of the carotid, a condition that was not life threatening and did not require surgery. Now he had in his hands the findings of another scan indicating a blockage of 80 percent. Additionally, there appeared to be an abdominal aneurysm. He decided that further evaluation, this time by a specialist, was needed.

The examination and testing conducted by the cardiologist confirmed the seriousness of Vince's medical situation. Not only was there significant blockage of the carotid artery (90 percent), but also blockage in three of Vince's coronary arteries. Both of these conditions posed a serious threat to his health. Vince would need to have surgery.

Although there would be two separate operations, the doctor offered to arrange for them to be conducted during the same hospitalization.

Vince entered the hospital on a Monday and had surgery—a carotid endarterectomy—performed on his right carotid artery the next day. Two days later his surgeon performed a quadruple bypass (once inside, the surgeon discovered a fourth blocked artery). Recovery from the second surgery was difficult for Vince, partly because his lungs had been weakened by fifty years of smoking. It was three days before he woke up and could have his breathing tube removed, and another four days before he was ready to return home.

Once Vince came home from the hospital, his recovery proceeded smoothly. Visits from his pastor and church members played an important part in his recovery, helping to keep his spirits up. So did the prayers they offered for him.

Two weeks after he left the hospital, Vince visited his cardiologist for a follow-up examination. The news was very encouraging: The surgeries had been successful. His heart and lungs were doing well. They were strong enough for him to get on a regular schedule of walking each day. A couple of weeks later Vince met with his surgeon for another evaluation and to discuss the other problem that had been detected by the Life Line screening—the abdominal aneurysm. Vince's surgeon listened to his heart and was happy with what he heard. The rhythm was good and strong. The incisions from the surgery were healing well too. He told Vince that he could start driving again. He also ordered another abdominal ultrasound in order to evaluate the aneurysm and to determine when the next surgery would need to be done.

A little more than a month later Vince again met with his surgeon. The doctor was pleased with Vince's continued progress. His heart was strong and the incisions had healed. In fact, he was healthy enough to undergo surgery to repair the aneurysm. This was fortunate, because the ultrasound revealed the aneurysm had grown two centimeters. Two weeks later the surgery was performed. This time during postoperative recovery he didn't need any mechanical assistance for his breathing. His lungs were stronger and he was able to breathe on his own. The five months without cigarettes had already paid off.

In less than a month Vince was out walking again every day, covering at least a mile each time. It was not long before he was ready to join a local fitness club, where he still continues to exercise on a regular basis. Now sixty-eight years old, Vince leads a healthy and vigorous life. It is a life that he appreciates considerably more than he did a few years ago, because he realizes how close he came to losing it. He also has a greater appreciation for the role a church can play in helping individuals maintain their health. He knows that his church gave him a wonderful gift by offering the screenings that detected his life-threatening conditions.

Vince realizes that he has a powerful testimony he can offer others. He knows that if he had not taken advantage of the health program offered at Trinity Lutheran, the first indication of his blocked arteries could have been a fatal stroke or heart attack. Even if he had survived the stroke or heart attack, he could have been seriously disabled for the rest of his life. This is why he is eager to stand before the congregation each year and make the announcement about the church's Life Line scans.

But Vince's determination to help others benefit from health screenings has reached beyond his own church. He shared his story with his sister, a member of a Catholic church in Fredericksburg, Virginia, and urged her to have the church offer a similar program. She, in turn, persuaded her priest to have Life Line come to their church. It was truly fortunate that they did. Vince's sister, one of the first to sign up for the scans, learned that she too had blockage in one of her carotid arteries. Additionally, when she went in for more extensive tests, she discovered significant blockages in three of her coronary arteries. Like her brother, she had believed that the absence of any symptoms meant she was in good health. It was only through the scans offered at her church that she learned she had a serious medical condition that required surgery.

These heartwarming accounts of church-sponsored programs saving the lives of Vince Grande and his sister would be incomplete if we didn't tell the story of how Vince's church first established its health ministry and how it has grown over the years.

Although Trinity Lutheran Church had addressed various health needs of the congregation and community for a number of years through occasional blood-pressure checks, blood drives, and educational programs, it did not have a coordinated program until 1997. That was the year that Pastor Peter Zieg received a letter from Florida Hospital asking if the church would be interested in developing a health ministry and if he knew of someone in his congregation who would like to be trained to lead this ministry. Well aware of the medical needs of many of his parishioners, Pastor Zieg felt that the time was right for the church to initiate a health ministry. He also felt confident that he knew the right person to take the lead in developing this program—Connie Brink.

Connie was an active and respected member of the congregation. Since joining the church in 1991, she had taught Sunday school and served on the worship and music committee, the fellowship committee, and the church council. As valuable as these contributions were, she was best known for her musical gifts. A professionally trained mezzo soprano, she touched the hearts of many in the congregation with her frequent solos.

Although Connie had carved out a successful musical career and wanted to remain active as a performer, in recent years she had felt called to use her talents in new ways. One talent that she realized she could draw on in another field was her ability to perform in front of groups. She felt comfortable and confident working with audiences, and she found it gratifying to see that her words and music were inspiring or comforting people.

Connie saw that she could use this strength to benefit others by becoming a health educator. She felt that she could be an articulate and persuasive teacher and help people learn how to enhance their health. To equip herself for this work, she returned to school and earned a master's degree in public health. She then took a position as a health educator for the county health department, serving a wide range of age groups, in a variety of settings. Through this work she had become well acquainted with the needs of the community and with the numerous resources that were available to residents.

Pastor Zieg felt that Connie's talents and training, combined with her commitment to serve others through her church, made her an ideal choice to participate in the hospital training program and then lead the development of a coordinated health ministry at the church. Connie shared Pastor Zieg's belief that the time was right for the church to move ahead with a health and healing ministry and that the Florida Hospital program could be exactly what was needed to launch it.

Connie was impressed by what she saw and heard during the Lay Health Educator workshops at the hospital. It was evident that Florida Hospital considered this an important program and was committed to providing training and ongoing support for the volunteers from local churches. Meeting in the boardroom of the hospital each week, volunteers were taught by an outstanding group of physicians, nurses, pharmacists, psychologists, chaplains, and other health professionals who were eager to share their knowledge.

Connie was also impressed with the other volunteers. Although none of them had the training she had in health care, it was obvious that they had an equally strong commitment to help others and to educate themselves about health issues that could be addressed in their churches. They wanted to learn about the steps they could advise people to take to reduce the risk of heart disease and cancer. They were excited to find out about hospital resources they could bring to their churches to help people detect high blood pressure or diabetes before these conditions could have devastating effects on their health. They were eager to learn how to reach out and help people who were suffering from depression or overwhelmed by caring for a loved one with Alzheimer's disease.

Connie's involvement in the program opened her eyes to what seemed like the almost unlimited potential of a congregational health ministry, and she saw how her own talents and experiences could be used more fully. Excited by what she had learned, she returned to her

church, ready to work with her pastor and other members to establish
a health ministry.

One of the first steps they took was to conduct a survey of church
members. The results revealed considerable interest in end-of-life issues. People wanted to know more about how they could maintain
control over the medical care they might be given. To address this interest, Connie arranged to bring in hospital experts to explain how
people could exercise their right to determine the treatments they
want by completing one or more advance directives, such as a living
will, a durable power of attorney for health care, and a do-not-resus-
citate order.

This was followed by the development of a program to train volunteers from the church to minister to members whose medical
problems limited their ability to leave home. Volunteers visited these
individuals to assist them with basic home care. For some they made
minor alterations in the home to reduce the risk of falls and accidents.
For others, they helped obtain and organize medications. And just as
important, they offered a ministry of presence.

It was also around this time that Pastor Zieg and Connie first obtained information about Life Line screening and decided that they
should arrange to bring the organization to their church. This, of
course, turned out to be a decision for which Vince Grande would
forever be thankful.

Trinity's health ministry added a new dimension shortly after Rev.
Jeff Cox joined the staff as associate pastor. Rev. Cox wholeheartedly
supported the work of the health ministry team, but he felt that the
church should also offer a healing service. In his previous pastorate
he had seen how meaningful it could be to parishioners. Working
closely with Pastor Zieg, Connie Brink, and other members of the
health ministry team, he designed a healing service that could be in-
corporated into the worship services on the Sundays communion was
offered.

The healing service was immediately embraced by the congregation and has become an important part of the worship service for

many who attend Trinity Lutheran Church. It is held on the first and third Sundays of each month. An announcement printed in the bulletin (and also read from the pulpit) tells worshipers that in addition to communion the church offers anointing with oil and laying on of hands for healing. It explains that individuals who wish to receive these can proceed to the back of the sanctuary after they have received communion. This invitation is generally accepted by at least twenty worshipers at each of the Sunday services. Additionally, the church holds a special healing service immediately after the worship service on the Sunday before Christmas for those who have lost a loved one during the year.

Trinity Lutheran's health ministry has continued to grow in interesting ways. In 2000 a community foundation gave Florida Hospital a grant to support the expansion of its work with congregations in central Florida. To handle this expanded program, the hospital needed a coordinator who had not only formal training in community health, but also a rich understanding and appreciation of religious congregations. Connie Brink quickly emerged as their choice for this position. Through her work at Trinity, Connie had demonstrated that she understood how to bring the resources of the medical community and those of a religious community together to create a dynamic health ministry.

Since joining the hospital staff as coordinator of the Lay Health Education program in her community, Connie has organized and led classes that have trained more than fifty volunteers from an ethnically and religiously diverse group of congregations. Working with these volunteers has been an uplifting experience for her. She reports that one of the most gratifying aspects has been witnessing people from different cultures and faith traditions work together and learn from each other. Often they form lasting relationships, insisting that they stay in touch not only with Connie but with each other as well.

Connie also has found it rewarding to help individuals who have no background in medicine but have a strong interest in serving others learn how to establish effective health ministries and to organize life-giving programs. Many of the volunteers in her classes reported that although they had felt called to serve as instruments of healing, they had not felt equipped to do so until they acquired the knowledge and resources provided by the hospital's training program. Working with these dedicated volunteers has been a transforming experience for Connie. She speaks freely of how it has enriched her life and strengthened her faith. And through this work she has become a part of a larger family of faith.

As Connie has helped other churches in her community develop health ministries, her own church's program has flourished. Several members of the congregation have been trained as Lay Health Educators. The health ministry team, now consisting of Pastor Cox, a registered nurse, a retired licensed practical nurse, a nursing student, the family and consumer scientist from the county, a dental hygienist, and a retired college instructor, is continually finding new ways to reach out to the congregation and the surrounding community. A column dedicated to health ministry now appears in the monthly newsletter mailed to the homes of all members. The health ministry team also places information about important health topics and medical services in bulletin inserts and on a board near the sanctuary.

Recently Trinity Lutheran obtained a grant from Wheat Ridge Ministries that will be used to support a program designed to help people make the lifestyle changes that will reduce their risk of developing heart disease. And the church continues to bring in guest speakers on health topics, often timing these presentations to coincide with awareness campaigns sponsored by national organizations, such as the American Heart Association, the American Cancer Society, and the Alzheimer's Association.

Pastor Zieg, Pastor Cox, Connie Brink, and the others who have provided leadership for the health ministry at Trinity Lutheran Church can look back over the past few years and rejoice. They know that the programs they organized have saved lives, enabled people to maintain their independence and dignity even as they faced debilitating chronic diseases, and provided emotional and spiritual support. But they also know that their work is just beginning. Fortunately, as they look ahead, they can see not only greater needs but also greater resources. More and more people are catching the exciting vision of the church carrying on the healing ministry of Christ through congregational health ministries.

Koenig's Corner

Members of our churches—younger and older, but especially retirees—have gifts and talents and experience acquired through years of service in the workplace. Lacking an opportunity to use these abilities, these people try to occupy their time with other activities—and they often grow bored in the process, while their special talents and abilities remain dormant and unused. The health ministries we've described provide these people with a way to use their talents to help others and at the same time enrich their own lives with purpose and meaning.

An increasing amount of scientific research is discovering that having a sense of meaning and purpose that comes from investing in the lives of others is what keeps a person's well-being high and physical health strong over the years. A sense of boredom or uselessness is a sure sign that one's talents are not being fully used, and it is one of the tasks of the church to ensure that human resources do not go to waste. As those resources are used more fully within health ministries, those in need will be cared for and those who provide that care will have fewer health needs.

It is essential to have key individuals in the congregation who are able to mobilize volunteers and train them for involvement in health ministries. This is the first step. What happened at Trinity Lutheran Church shows how God calls and prepares people like Vince, Pastor Cox, and Connie within congregations precisely for this purpose. It takes visionary leadership by the pastor and staff to create an environment where this can happen.

Strokes—Some Basic Information

- Each year approximately 700,000 Americans suffer a stroke.
- Stroke is the third leading cause of death in the United States, accounting for more than 150,000 deaths each year.
- It is the leading cause of serious disability.
- More than half of all strokes could be prevented.
- The risk of stroke increases significantly with age.
- The risk is greater in people who have close relatives who have had a stroke.
- African Americans and Hispanics have a greater risk of death and disability from stroke.
- The single greatest risk factor is high blood pressure.
- Cigarette smoking increases the risk of stroke.
- Individuals with diabetes have an increased risk of stroke.
- When the warning signs of a stroke appear, immediate medical attention is absolutely essential.

What Can Be Done in Your Congregation

- Conduct regular blood-pressure screenings before or after worship services.
- Sponsor ultrasound scans to detect blockage in the carotid artery.
- Distribute information about symptoms. According to the National Stroke Association, the five most common symptoms are:
  - sudden numbness or weakness of the face, arm, or leg, especially on one side of the body
  - sudden confusion, trouble speaking or understanding
  - sudden trouble seeing in one or both eyes
  - sudden trouble walking, dizziness, loss of balance or coordination
  - sudden severe headache with no known cause

- Provide regular reminders of the importance of seeking emergency medical treatment at the first sign of stroke symptoms.
- For individuals who require rehabilitation after a stroke, offer support and assistance to them and their families.

chapter four

An Unmistakable Sign

The members of First Presbyterian Church of DeLand, Florida, were full of hope and enthusiasm as they entered the sanctuary for the eleven o'clock worship service on the third Sunday of November in 1998. They were looking forward to the beginning of a new chapter in the life of the church. The previous chapter had been disappointing and even painful at times. It had included disagreements and conflict that drove many members away. Attendance at Sunday worship services had dropped to only half of what it had been a few years before. Now, with their new minister ready to preach his first sermon, members were eager to embark on a new phase.

For Rev. Bruce Hedgepeth, this was something of a homecoming. He had grown up in the suburbs of Chicago, but his college years had been spent in DeLand at Stetson University. It had been a very positive and meaningful time for him. Stetson had provided him with academic challenges and opportunities that allowed him to grow intellectually and to gain confidence in his abilities. The university had also afforded him the opportunity to establish valuable relationships, many of which had endured for more than a decade. One relationship that was particularly important was the one with Cindy Gilliland; it had led to marriage and a family that now included two children, Will and Kate.

The small-college atmosphere had also enabled Bruce to establish a personal connection with several of his professors, and he

often sought them out for counsel on important concerns. Now, he
realized, he would be serving as the pastor for some of these same
professors.

As Rev. Hedgepeth sat in the chancel and thought about the worship service that was about to begin, he also reflected on the path that
had brought him back to DeLand. It certainly seemed that God had
led him along the path. He had been completely satisfied with his position as an associate pastor at another Presbyterian church and was
not looking to move. Nonetheless, when he was asked to apply for the
position in DeLand, he felt that there must be a reason for the invitation and that he should consider it. From that point on, all the signs
seemed to point toward DeLand. Now he was here, and it was almost
time to begin the worship service.

Only moments before Rev. Hedgepeth was to step into the pulpit,
he was approached by the head usher and informed that there was a
serious medical emergency in the back of the sanctuary and that
emergency medical services had been called. Although his seminary
training had not prepared him for this situation, he recalled a time
that he had been in a worship service and a similar crisis had developed. Remembering how the minister at that service had handled the
situation, he stood and spoke to the congregation in a serious but
calm voice, informing them that a medical emergency had arisen. He
asked that any physicians or other medical professionals in the congregation who might be able to provide assistance until the emergency rescue team arrived move quickly to the back of the sanctuary
to see if they could be of help. He then asked that the rest of the congregation sit quietly and pray.

There were two physicians in the congregation that day, and both
responded immediately to Rev. Hedgepeth's announcement. Upon
arriving at the back of the sanctuary, they found John Orr slumped
over in the pew next to his wife. He had gone into cardiac arrest. He
would need to be resuscitated immediately if he were to have a chance
of surviving. Neither doctor had been called on to perform cardiopulmonary resuscitation in many years, but they were ready to
begin when a woman came hurrying back and climbed over the pew

in front of John Orr. She promptly began CPR with such skill and authority that it was obvious to both doctors that John Orr's heart and life were in good hands. It was only later they learned that she was a nurse who worked in the cardiac care unit of a hospital in Tallahassee, and that her only reason for being in church in DeLand that day, at least as far as she knew, was to witness the baptism of her grandson.

Minutes later the emergency medical technicians arrived and took over. Using a defibrillator, they were able to get John's heart to start beating on its own again. He was now ready to be moved to the ambulance and transported to the hospital for more extensive medical care.

Having given John Orr over into the care of medical professionals and having blessed him on his way to the hospital, the new pastor spoke the call to worship and, in the emotionally and spiritually charged atmosphere of the morning, set in motion both the morning worship service and his ministry in DeLand. The service proceeded as planned, with the addition of a special prayer for John and Alice Marie Orr, but no one in the congregation could forget the frightening scene that had occurred. The Orrs remained in the thoughts and prayers of worshipers throughout the service, with everyone hoping that there would be good news from the hospital. Fortunately, by the end of the service, there was encouraging news that Rev. Hedgepeth could report to the congregation. He had received word that John Orr was breathing on his own and was in stable condition. Later in the day friends at church learned that John would need to be transferred to another hospital on Monday where a pacemaker and internal defibrillator would be implanted, but that he should be able to return home in a few days.

The events of November 15 left a deep impression on the new minister and the members of First Presbyterian Church. What had happened at the beginning of Rev. Hedgepeth's inaugural worship service was dramatic evidence that the church needed to be attuned to the physical as well as the spiritual dimension of the lives of its members. But there were less dramatic aspects to John Orr's illness that also illustrated the need for the church to care for the body and the mind as well as the soul. As wonderful as it was that John had been brought back to life in the sanctuary and was able to return home after only a few days in the hospital, he and Alice Marie still faced a number of physical and emotional challenges. Although John had periods during which he was able to attend worship services and other church functions or to enjoy special times with his family, there were other times when chronic medical problems seriously restricted his activities.

One of the most serious challenges came when John's kidneys failed and he needed to have dialysis treatments at home. Handling the equipment and supplies for this put a tremendous physical strain on Alice Marie. John also had to return to the hospital for several stays and eventually had to move to a nursing home. This left Alice Marie home alone for lengthy periods, isolated and in need of occasional help with some basic chores, such as cleaning branches and trash out of the yard. The youth leaders at the church, Megan and David Collins, learned of her need for assistance with the yard work and arranged for some of the members of the youth group at the church to help. Out of this developed a relationship that continued until Megan and David left for seminary. They would stop by to visit Alice Marie on a regular basis, often bringing along lunch. She credits their visits and prayers with helping to lift her spirits during this lonely period.

It was visits of friends from the church that also kept up John's spirits during these challenging times. He was no longer able to serve on the stewardship committee and assist with church finances as he had before, but he liked to be kept abreast of developments at the church. And he enjoyed reminiscing with some of his longtime friends from the church about earlier days.

The health-related challenges faced by John and Alice Marie Orr provided compelling evidence of the need for their church to develop a ministry of health and healing. This new chapter in the life and ministry of First Presbyterian Church needed to include a better means of addressing the various health concerns of its members and the community it served.

Fortunately, the seeds of a health ministry had already been planted. Two members, Marshall and Marie Moser, had participated in the same Lay Health Educator training program as had Nancy Force of Westminster-by-the-Sea Presbyterian Church. The Mosers brought to their health ministry extensive backgrounds in education. Marshall had worked in a variety of positions in the Grosse Pointe, Michigan, school system for twenty-five years, including several years as a principal, before retiring to Florida. Still full of energy and concern for young people, he worked for a few more years in a school system in the greater Orlando area before retiring for a second time. Marie's initial training was in nursing, but she too felt the call to help guide young people as they prepared for their adult years. She returned to college to obtain a teaching degree and then served as the director of a program in an Orlando area high school that prepared students for careers in the health field.

Like so many other church members who are retired and no longer bound by the constraints of a set work schedule, Marshall and Marie were eager to find new and creative outlets for their altruism. For them, there was nothing more gratifying than to identify important human needs and then find ways to help people meet those needs. They were active in other community organizations that allowed them to help others, but it was the church where they felt they could contribute the most, and they welcomed the opportunity to take the initiative in a health ministry.

One of the concerns Marshall and Marie heard expressed frequently by church members, especially the more senior members, focused on end-of-life medical care. They knew of individuals who, incapacitated by serious injury or illness, had been unable to determine the type and extent of medical care they received in their final days. Sometimes decisions about care had to be made by their families or the hospital. Often families, unprepared for this situation, would find themselves in conflict about what should be done and feeling guilty about whichever choice they finally made. There were no easy answers to questions such as "What is best for our mother?" or "What would she have wanted?" And in cases where there were no relatives to step in and make these decisions, they were made by doctors or hospital staff who hardly knew the patients and had no sense of what the patients would have chosen. Sometimes decisions were contrary to what the patient's closest friends knew the patient would have wanted, but even close friends were powerless to influence the decisions.

Through the Lay Health Educator program, Marshall and Marie had learned that there were some rather simple steps people could take to avoid these situations. By clearly communicating their wishes to their doctors and family members and by completing some uncomplicated forms that gave directions or authority to others, they could maintain control over major medical decisions, even if they were unconscious. Marshall and Marie realized that this was exactly the type of information their fellow parishioners needed, and they decided this would be the subject of their first congregational health program.

Held in the fellowship hall of First Presbyterian, the program was led by Paula Morton, a social worker from the community hospital, and Dan Vaughen, an attorney who was also a member of the church. More than fifty people came to the program, where they heard Paula give examples of difficult medical situations that individuals had encountered and the decisions that had to be made about their care. She discussed the rules and procedures that the hospital was required to follow in these situations. She emphasized that even when doctors and nurses thought they knew what the patient wanted, they might be required to follow a different course if they did not have written directions from the patient.

Paula and Dan then explained how people could maintain control over these situations. They stressed that patients *always* had the right to make important decisions about their medical care, and that this right could be exercised even if they were incapacitated by an illness or injury. They could do this by simply completing a couple of forms. The first would be a living will. This document would allow them to specify which treatments they would or would not want should they become incapacitated and be terminally ill or in a persistent vegetative state without a probability of recovery. They then discussed a durable power of attorney for health care. This document would allow them to appoint a family member or friend to act as their agent (sometimes called a health care surrogate or surrogate decision maker) and make decisions about medical care should they become incapacitated.

The questions that followed the presentations revealed a high degree of interest in the subject. Many in the audience said they had completed living wills but were unfamiliar with the durable power of attorney for health care. They wanted to know more about what they should consider as they selected a surrogate decision maker. There were also questions about what individuals could do to be certain that the doctors and hospitals would know they had completed these forms and that their directives would be followed. This led to a discussion about the importance of people talking with both their health care providers and family members about these documents and their feelings regarding end-of-life care. Several individuals in the audience, understanding for the first time the importance of advance directives, asked how they could obtain or prepare these forms. They were pleased to learn that Paula and Dan had brought copies with them and were willing to assist individuals who wanted to complete them.

It was clear to Marshall and Marie that the program on advance directives had met an important need within the congregation. People were concerned about losing control over decisions regarding their medical care, and they appreciated being given the knowledge and tools that would allow them to maintain that control. Additionally, several commented on how meaningful it was to have this discussion on end-of-life issues held in a church rather than a hospital auditorium. For them, church was exactly where such issues should be addressed.

While losing control over medical decisions was a serious concern to many, there were those who felt that a more immediate issue was loss of control over their daily lives and the stress they experienced as they rushed to accomplish everything they felt they needed to do.

People felt overwhelmed by the various and often competing responsibilities they had. There never seemed to be enough time for all the things they needed to do, and often they felt pulled in three or four different directions. With too many responsibilities and too little time, they felt physically and emotionally drained at the end of the day. For some, the harmful effects of stress were far greater. Their doctors had warned them that stress was damaging their bodies and increasing their risk of developing serious health problems. They were advised to find ways to reduce stress or, at least, to manage it more effectively.

Marshall and Marie were familiar enough with the congregation to sense that stress was a serious issue for many. Working in collaboration with two volunteers from the nearby Baptist church who had also completed the Lay Health Education program, they organized a workshop on stress management. This workshop, led by a mental health professional from the hospital, provided participants with some of the strategies and tools they needed to reduce stress and regain control over their lives. Participation required a careful self-examination. Those joining in the workshop were asked to articulate and affirm their values and then to analyze their priorities. Then, with the guidance of the workshop leader, they looked closely at the points at which their values and priorities intersected and they considered whether adjusting their schedule and realigning their priorities might put them back in control and reduce stress in their lives. The workshop had its practical, immediately useful side also: Participants were taught relaxation techniques they could use to calm their minds and relax their bodies during periods of unavoidable stress.

The reactions of participants were overwhelmingly positive. They left with a clearer understanding of what was creating stress in their lives and greater confidence in their ability to manage it more effectively.

The success of the programs on end-of-life medical care and stress management provided evidence of the interest in church-sponsored health programs. It was becoming increasingly clear that First Presbyterian needed to develop more programs that focused on health and healing, and that the church could play an important role in linking people with appropriate medical resources. The church, through educational programs and preventive interventions, could empower people to take control of their health and health care and to take care of each other as well.

Rev. Hedgepeth and church leaders decided that one way to address this need would be to incorporate health topics and activities in established church programs. One of the first offerings was a five-week class on the faith-health connection, presented as part of the Wednesday-evening adult education series. Students in this class had the opportunity to explore the growing empirical evidence of a relationship between religious involvement and positive health outcomes. They learned about the fascinating research of Herbert Benson, David Larson, Jeffrey Levin, and Dale Matthews, among others.

A subsequent Wednesday-evening series brought in guest speakers to talk about common health problems. A cardiologist spoke on heart disease, highlighting the steps people could take to reduce their risk of heart disease and answering questions about various treatment options. A family practitioner spoke on hypertension, clarifying misconceptions about the condition and offering information on treatment approaches. Depression was the subject of another program, with a psychologist sharing information on psychological and medical treatments. Another psychologist came in the following week to do a program on stress management.

Response to these two series was so positive that additional programs were offered. A dermatologist gave a presentation on skin cancer, emphasizing the actions people could take to prevent it. A dietitian led a program on nutrition and health. A presentation on travel medicine was offered by a nurse from the church who had become knowledgeable on the subject through her experience on several mission trips to Latin America.

The church also arranged for on-site screenings that could help members uncover medical conditions that might not have produced any symptoms. There were blood-pressure checks and scans that could detect a heightened risk of strokes. As flu season approached, information about the importance of flu vaccinations was disseminated.

The interest of church members in these programs has continued to grow, and so has the commitment of church leaders to make health ministries an integral part of the church's life and mission. Rev. Hedgepeth recently reported, "Church leadership recognizes the importance of congregational health ministries. We have decided that this work should be an integral part of our caregiving ministries. To that end, our board of deacons (the designated organizers of caregiving) has health ministries as a regular part of its responsibilities. We have recently hosted a blood drive and are currently investigating the possibility of partnering with a neighboring church and local hospital to add a parish nurse to our staff. We see clearly that these ministries increase our ability to care for others in Jesus's name."

Koenig's Corner

There are so many ways that faith communities can contribute to the health and well-being of their members. With congregations aging (more than half of the membership of mainline churches is now over age sixty), it becomes more and more important to be prepared for emergencies in church; to help members and their families make end-of-life decisions; to facilitate health promotion activities such as skin cancer prevention, stress management, nutrition education, blood pressure checks, and flu vaccinations; and to screen for diabetes, elevated cholesterol, and prostate and colon cancer. It was the church that introduced into modern history the notion of "caring for the sick" that ultimately led to the building of hospitals. Now, there's a critical need to prevent illness and maintain health, as our medical resources are quickly diminishing and the need for such resources is greatly expanding. This presents the church with an opportunity to make a real difference not only in the lives of its own members, but also in the surrounding community. This is what loving my neighbor is all about.

Heart Disease—Some Basic Information

- Heart disease is the number one killer of American men and women, accounting for more than 700,000 deaths each year.
- Risk factors for heart disease include:
  - diabetes
  - elevated total and LDL cholesterol levels
  - high blood pressure
  - smoking
  - obesity
  - physical inactivity

What Can Be Done in Your Congregation

- Distribute American Heart Association information about the warning signs of a heart attack:
  - chest discomfort that lasts more than a few minutes or that goes away and comes back
  - pain or discomfort in one or both arms, the back, neck, jaw, or stomach
  - shortness of breath
  - breaking out in a cold sweat, nausea, or lightheadedness
- Distribute American Heart Association information about signs of cardiac arrest:
  - sudden loss of responsiveness, no response to gentle shaking
  - no normal breathing—the victim does not take a normal breath when you check for several seconds
  - no signs of circulation, no movement or coughing
- Offer classes in cardiopulmonary resuscitation (CPR).
- Investigate obtaining an automated external defibrillator for the church.
- Sponsor a walking group or other programs to encourage members to increase physical activity.

Advanced Directives—Some Basic Information

- Every adult has the right to make decisions about the nature and extent of his or her medical care. Advance directives allow individuals to maintain control over these decisions even if they are incapacitated by injury or illness.
- A living will allows people to specify which treatments they would or would not want should they become incapacitated and be terminally ill or in a persistent vegetative state.
- A durable power of attorney for health care allows persons to appoint another individual to make decisions about medical treatments should they become incapacitated and unable to make or communicate their own decisions.
- Since it is impossible for people to foresee all the medical situations they might encounter, it is advisable for everyone to complete a living will and a durable power of attorney for health care—or a health care advance directive that combines these two into a single document.

What Can Be Done in Your Congregation

- Organize a church forum on end-of-life issues and advance directives. Forum participants could include a member of the clergy, a hospital social worker, a physician or nurse, and an attorney.
- Use bulletin inserts and church mailings to provide members with basic information about advance directives and copies of sample forms.
- Encourage members to share their thoughts and decisions about end-of-life care with their families.

chapter five

Sharing One Another's Burdens

Winnie Boyle was panic-stricken. She had taken a brief break from her nursing duties at the hospital to call home to check on her husband, Jim, but had been unable to reach him. She knew he should be home, and she had let the phone ring long enough to give him plenty of time to pick it up. She called several more times. There was still no answer. Where was he? What could have happened to him? The image that came into her mind and stayed there as she asked herself these questions was one of Jim lying on the floor, dead or seriously injured from a fall. She felt she had to check on him immediately. After quickly explaining the situation to her supervisor, she raced home, fearing all the way what she would find when she got there.

When Winnie arrived home, she called out for Jim as soon as she opened the door. She was greatly relieved when she heard his voice, but then she realized there was a serious problem. He could not move. He was frozen in a chair, unable to answer the phone or call for help, and he had been in this rigid state for more than an hour. The Parkinson's disease that had first been diagnosed more than a decade ago had, at this moment, a complete hold over his body.

Jim and Winnie Boyle's struggle with Parkinson's disease began fourteen years earlier, in 1973. Jim had moved to Florida from Ohio the year before to take a new job. He had brought their five children with him to get them started in their new schools while Winnie stayed behind to sell their house. As soon as their house sold, Winnie joined Jim and the children. It was while she was still getting settled in their new house in Florida that she noticed something about Jim that concerned her. Although he seemed to be in good health and did not complain of any symptoms, she noticed that he dragged one of his feet as he walked. Her first thought was that this might be caused by a brain tumor, and she insisted that he go to the hospital for tests.

They were relieved to learn that the tests showed no evidence of a brain tumor, but the news was not entirely good. The doctors had concluded that Jim had Parkinson's disease. Although the symptoms were mild enough that Jim could continue working, they knew that eventually the disease would dramatically alter both of their lives.

Fortunately, the next few years were largely uneventful medically. In spite of some new symptoms, Jim was able to continue in his job as a purchasing agent, and Winnie was able to continue working as a nurse, a profession she loved dearly. Their life was full. Most of the time apart from their jobs was devoted to their daughter and four sons. Lifelong Catholics, Winnie and Jim were also active in their church.

By 1980, Jim's symptoms were becoming more serious and were beginning to limit his ability to carry out some of his work responsibilities and participate in many normal family activities. He had less and less control over his leg and foot, and his gait was affected. This in turn led to severe back problems that required surgery. Unfortunately, he was unable to return to work for very long afterward.

As the disease progressed, there were times that the lower half of Jim's body would freeze. On several occasions this had happened in a restaurant or other public setting. No matter how much he tried to will his legs and feet to move, they would remain motionless. Sometimes the only way he could get moving again was by having family members hold him and rock him back and forth from heel to toe. Reluctantly, Winnie and Jim acknowledged that the time had come for him to retire. They were concerned, however, that he would need to stay home by himself while Winnie continued to work full-time at the hospital.

Although Winnie was never entirely comfortable leaving Jim home by himself for long periods, this arrangement seemed to work satisfactorily. Jim was still able to take care of many of the household chores and errands, and he enjoyed reading and listening to music. And since they lived near their church, he could attend Mass every day. If minor problems arose, there were family and neighbors nearby who could be called.

This arrangement, which permitted Winnie to work in the profession she felt called to and at the same time allowed Jim the sense of independence that becomes especially important when it is threatened, was in fact quite satisfactory—until the frightening episode in 1987 made it clear that it was no longer safe for Jim to stay by himself for long periods. He would need to have others around to provide some assistance and to come to his aid if another emergency arose. But it was not clear to Winnie and Jim how to arrange this, since they could not afford for Winnie to give up her job. They needed to find someplace safe he could stay while she was at work. Winnie began checking in the community to see what was available for people in their situation. There did not, however, seem to be any facility or program that would meet their needs. Finally, Winnie found a partial solution. There was an Alzheimer's disease respite program that would take Jim for three days each week.

The Alzheimer's respite program provided some relief, but it was not what either Jim or Winnie wanted. They both felt that there must be something better and more appropriate for his medical condition. Then, as if in answer to their prayers, St. Mary Magdalen Catholic Church announced that it would soon be opening an adult day care center. The suggestion for this center had come from two members of the church, a retired physician and his wife, both of whom had a long-standing interest in the needs of older adults. Acting on their suggestion, St. Mary Magdalen had formed a committee to study the matter and to survey the congregation. When the committee concluded that there was a need for such a program, the church decided to move ahead with a plan to establish the adult center. Soon there would be a place for families to safely leave their loved ones who needed special care.

The church chose one of its members, Annette Kelly, to be the first director of the center. Annette was a registered nurse who had worked for a number of years with older adults. Particularly important in her preparation for this task was the valuable experience she gained by taking care of a terminally ill relative in her home. She knew what it was like to have round-the-clock caregiving responsibilities. Another church member who was also a nurse, Phyllis Fox, was hired as assistant director.

With Annette and Phyllis leading the way, the adult center began to take shape. By the spring of 1987, it was ready to serve members of the parish and other faith communities as well. The first client to come through the door of the center was Jim Boyle. This arrangement was ideal for Winnie and Jim. Winnie could bring Jim to the center every morning on her way to the hospital and then pick him up as she returned home, and while at work she could enjoy peace of mind, knowing that he was secure and safe.

Although protecting their clients was paramount in the minds of Annette and Phyllis, they wanted the center to offer more than just a sheltered environment. They wanted to create a physical and social setting that celebrated the personhood of each participant. The fact that a person could no longer live independently did not mean that he or she should be treated as any less of a person. For the staff of the adult center, this meant that they needed to know each client's interests and habits. For example, in Jim's case it meant that someone met him at the door each morning with a newspaper and cup of coffee. And when they learned that one of his favorite hobbies was playing bridge, they found volunteers from the church who also enjoyed bridge and who were willing to play with him, allowing him to take as long as he needed. In this and other ways, the professional staff and volunteers lovingly accommodated his limitations.

The physical location and layout of the center offered many features not found in most institutional settings for the elderly or impaired. The church had wisely decided to place the center in the middle of the church complex. This meant that participants in the adult center would be able to see people of all ages as they involved themselves in the various programs and activities offered at the church. With the child center next door, the adult center participants could watch the young parents bringing their children to the center in the morning and coming back for them later in the day. Occasionally the staff from the child center would bring over an infant, giving clients a chance to admire and gently rock a young child again. Every Monday, preschool students would visit, and on Tuesdays and Thursdays there would be an intergenerational program involving students from the elementary school. Frequently the church youth group would come by to present special programs.

Jim and the other clients could also spend some of their time sitting in the sunshine on the patio. From there they could see and hear young children on the playground, laughing with joy as they flew through the air on their swings or came breezing down the slide. Looking out a little farther, they could see the students from the church's school playing on the athletic fields or practicing with the band. They could also see the people attending the various events held in the parish life center, and often they were able to attend these programs themselves. There they could listen to the musical performances of school groups or wander among the displays at the science fair. What a difference these extra benefits made in the lives of these adults whose impairment was robbing them of health-sustaining human contact. Such benefits, rarely attainable in a secular setting, were readily available in the setting of a church campus.

The lives of the clients were also enriched by the work of volunteers from the church. Their contributions allowed the center to offer clients more individual attention and a greater variety of activities. One parishioner stopped by regularly with his ham radio. He would sit with clients on the patio and tune in other ham radio operators around the country, and then mark their locations on a map. Another parishioner, a young schoolteacher, would drop by along with her child one afternoon each week to lead a reading group. A businessman would visit regularly to review major news stories of the week. Other volunteers came to the center to assist with gardening or various arts and crafts.

Of course, there is also a spiritual dimension to the center. For people of faith, and especially for the members of St. Mary Magdalen and other Catholic parishes in the region, the center enables them to continue their religious practices. Every Tuesday and Friday, a Eucharistic minister comes to the center and offers communion, and on Wednesdays a member of the parish leads interested clients through the rosary. There is also a monthly Mass celebrated at the center by one of the priests.

There are other opportunities for clients to nurture their faith. For those who want a quiet place to pray or meditate, the church is only a few steps from the center. Nearby there is also a prayer garden and grotto with a statue of Mary. In the garden there is a wandering path that has stones along the way, each engraved with some lines of poetry written by the former bishop of the diocese.

St. Mary Magdalen reaches out in other ways as well to families who need the adult center. Many of the clients in the center are suffering from Alzheimer's disease, the progressive neurological disease that eventually places tremendous burdens on family caregivers. Although the adult center provides respite care during the day, family caregivers still have responsibility for the evenings and nights. This is a responsibility that can be emotionally and physically exhausting. Caregivers often need the understanding and support of others who are going through similar experiences. To help these people, the adult center works closely with the Alzheimer's Association. One evening a month the Alzheimer's Association sponsors a caregiver support group that meets at St. Mary Magdalen. Here family members can come together to share their frustrations and concerns and to offer each other love and support.

One of the most difficult issues many of these caregivers eventually face is deciding when to place their loved one in a more comprehensive care setting. Although one of the primary goals of the adult center is to delay or even preclude placement in a nursing home, for many clients the time comes when more intensive or comprehensive care is required. When that time arrives, the center's staff works closely with the client and family to find the best setting and to ease the transition.

The move to a nursing home or assisted-living facility is also aided by another program offered at St. Mary Magdalen. More than two hundred members of the congregation participate in the church's ministry to the sick. These lay ministers first complete diocesan training and receive certification. Once trained and commissioned by the diocese, they regularly call on parishioners who are in residential facilities and unable to attend services held at the church. Pastoral care for these parishioners living in nursing homes or assisted-living facilities is also provided by the priests of St. Mary Magdalen, who visit on the first Friday of each month. During these visits they celebrate Mass and administer the sacrament of anointing.

The loving and compassionate care provided by the ministries of St. Mary Magdalen carried Jim and Winnie Boyle through their most difficult periods. For Jim, the adult center not only provided a safe and secure setting each day; it did so in a way that allowed him to maintain his dignity and individuality. It also gave him the opportunity to find strength and meaning in the religious practices that were so important to him. For Winnie, the center enabled her to continue in her position as a hospital nurse, a position that provided financial support for the family and the sense of professional accomplishment she needed. When Jim's symptoms became more severe, Annette and Phyllis helped Winnie and Jim find a good nursing home. And, near the end of Jim's life, when Winnie feared that she would not be emotionally able to handle his death, a counselor at the church helped her find the strength she needed.

In recent years, a large number of churches in central Florida have recognized the need to provide support and guidance for their members who are facing the same challenges that confronted Jim and Winnie Boyle. Church leaders have become aware of the difficult decisions and limited options these individuals face when a loved one has been diagnosed with Alzheimer's disease, Parkinson's disease, or another debilitating chronic condition. They have heard parishioners voice their desire to care for their loved ones at home rather than place them in a nursing home, and they have seen the tremendous strain these parishioners experience when they assume full-time caregiving responsibilities.

One way many of these churches have addressed this challenge is to work together in a community-wide program known as Share the Care. Initially organized as the Alzheimer's Respite Care Program, this service started as a division of the Christian Service Center of Central Florida, a nonprofit, nondenominational organization. Now an independent organization that remains physically and philosophically close to the Christian Service Center, Share the Care provides a wide range of services to individuals of all faiths who are struggling with the demands of Alzheimer's disease and other life-limiting conditions.

Sometimes the most confusing challenge caregivers face initially is obtaining an accurate diagnosis. They know that their loved one is having memory problems, but they don't know if he or she has Alzheimer's disease. In these cases, Share the Care will arrange an appointment with a neurologist at a memory disorders clinic affiliated with a medical center. Share the Care can also arrange to have a social worker assist with the paperwork and be present when the doctor explains the diagnosis.

Another valuable service offered by Share the Care is care management. A professional care manager is available to meet with individuals and families to assess their situation and to discuss various resources and options. Following this assessment, the care manager can help the family develop a comprehensive care plan and put it into action. Sometimes one of the first steps family members need to take is to improve their caregiving skills. If this is the case, then Share the Care can provide the training.

Another service that Share the Care offers is in-home counseling. Caregivers are at high risk for depression. Fortunately, the support and problem-solving strategies an experienced counselor provides can often help caregivers manage the stresses and strains of their responsibilities without sinking into a depression. Recognizing that many caregivers cannot leave home to get to a counselor's office, Share the Care has counselors who can provide their services in the caregivers' homes.

Share the Care also operates two licensed adult day care centers. These centers, one adjoining the Christian Service Center in downtown Orlando and the other at St. Luke's United Methodist Church in south Orlando, are open from 7:30 to 5:30 Monday through Friday. Many of the clients are brought there by family members who need to continue working but want to be assured that their loved one is well cared for. Other clients come to the day care centers primarily because they enjoy and benefit from being around other people. Like the adult center at St. Mary Magdalen, these centers rely on both professional staff and volunteers to create a setting that provides loving care and that respects the dignity of all clients. Volunteers from churches also add a spiritual dimension to these programs. For example, every Thursday one of the sponsoring churches sends volunteers to lead a religious service that is offered as an option to the clients.

Some caregivers find that they do not require extensive day care services but occasionally need a few hours away to take care of business matters or visit with friends. Share the Care helps these individuals by sponsoring four neighborhood respite sites, located in churches and community centers, that provide up to six hours of care one or two days per week. Another option available to caregivers with limited needs is in-house respite care. In this program, Share the Care offers caregivers a break by sending a trained companion to the house to stay with their loved one for a few hours.

Share the Care can also help families make modifications to their home to accommodate a wheelchair or other equipment. They will send workers who can build ramps, widen doorways, and install railings.

Still other challenges may be encountered by caregivers for frail elderly persons or individuals with Alzheimer's disease. They may have their own medical emergency or need to travel out of town to respond to a family emergency. Anticipating such situations, Share the Care has made arrangements with several assisted-living facilities to take in clients on a short-term basis.

Even with all the support that Share the Care provides, caregivers often need a total break from their responsibilities and some time to renew themselves. Share the Care has developed a creative program that addresses this need. Once a year they sponsor a caregiver forum. This three-day, two-night retreat, held at a hotel, is entirely free for the caregivers. Additionally, free respite care is provided for their loved ones. For these three days, caregivers are free to relax and enjoy the food, entertainment, and speakers provided by Share the Care. An increasingly popular and appreciated event, the most recent forum attracted more than three hundred caregivers.

Share the Care extends its reach even further by working closely with other organizations in the community, including the local chapter of the Alzheimer's Association. When people in the community call the Alzheimer's Association seeking information about services for individuals and families affected by Alzheimer's disease, Share the Care is one of the programs they are encouraged to call. Interestingly, the voice on the phone offering this suggestion is likely to be that of Winnie Boyle, the same Winnie Boyle who years ago experienced the desperation and helplessness people feel when they first learn a loved one has a progressive neurological disease. It is also interesting to note that the director of the Alzheimer's Association is Annette Kelly. These two women, who first came together at the adult center at St. Mary Magdalen Catholic Church, one as the director and the other as a caregiver in need of help, are reunited and working together to help the growing numbers of people throughout central Florida affected by Alzheimer's disease.

There are other ways that the religious community and secular organizations like the Alzheimer's Association collaborate to meet the needs of families. Families often turn first to their clergy after learning that a loved one has Alzheimer's disease. To be helpful to these parishioners, clergy need to have an accurate understanding of the disease and knowledge of community resources. They can obtain this information and stay updated through workshops offered on a regular basis by Annette Kelly and the Alzheimer's Association. The

Alzheimer's Association also provides training for facilitators for the caregiver support groups, many of which meet in churches.

There is no question that the adult center at St. Mary Magdalen Catholic Church and the programs offered by Share the Care have benefited from the inspired and creative leadership of compassionate and caring professionals. But none of these programs could have been successful were it not for the countless hours given by volunteers from the churches. These programs have succeeded because they have given Christians a means of putting their faith into action. They have offered people of faith the magnificent opportunity to participate in the work of God. And those who have participated invariably report that they have found their own faith strengthened and enriched. They have learned that true worship is not limited to sermons, songs, and prayer. Such programs as the one at St. Mary Magdalen have taught them that worship may also be what you do out there in the world that needs compassionate deeds far more than it needs words.

Koenig's Corner

Share the Care is yet another example of how one or more religious institutions can not only meet the health care needs of sick members and their families, but also make a significant contribution to the surrounding community. It takes visionary leadership by one person, often someone whose own life has been touched by chronic illness.

The aging of the population of the United States and other developed countries around the world will soon create huge health care needs. If we consider Alzheimer's disease alone, by the year 2050, the number of cases will exceed 14 million, nearly four times the number currently.[1] As noted earlier in this book, community hospitals could

1. Based on aged population projected for 2050 (U.S. Census 2000) and current rates of Alzheimer's disease estimated at 47 percent of those aged eighty-five or older; see D. A. Evans et al., *Journal of the American Medical Association* 262 (1989): 2551–56.

start looking like intensive care units, nursing homes could start to resemble community hospitals, and consequently, all of the rest of health care would back up into people's homes. We are already seeing these trends in our health care institutions, and they are likely to escalate dramatically in the future as our elderly population doubles or possibly even triples over the next half-century. More and more people will need to be cared for in their homes by family caregivers, and many of these people will be members of churches.

As health care for the elderly and disabled moves more and more into the community, and religious institutions are called to help meet the need, model programs like St. Mary Magdalen and Share the Care provide a blueprint that others can follow.

Alzheimer's Disease—Some Basic Information

- Alzheimer's disease is the most common form of dementia, affecting approximately 4 million Americans.
- It is estimated that as many as 10 percent of persons over the age of sixty-five and almost 50 percent of those over the age of eighty-five have Alzheimer's disease.
- Alzheimer's disease progresses at widely varying rates, with the time from the onset of symptoms until death ranging from three to twenty years; the average duration is about eight years.
- Patients should have a thorough diagnostic examination to rule out other disorders because memory problems caused by treatable conditions—such as depression or adverse drug reactions—are sometimes mistaken for Alzheimer's disease.
- The risk of Alzheimer's disease is greater if there is a family history of the illness.
- High cholesterol and high blood pressure may increase the risk of developing Alzheimer's disease.
- Although there is no known cure for Alzheimer's disease, there are some medications that can often produce modest improvements in memory and cognitive skills.

• Family caregivers are at a greatly increased risk of depression.

What Can Be Done in Your Congregation

• Publish the Alzheimer's Association's ten warning signs of Alzheimer's disease:
  • memory loss
  • difficulty performing familiar tasks
  • problems with language
  • disorientation to time and place
  • poor or decreased judgment
  • problems with abstract thinking
  • misplacing things
  • changes in mood or behavior
  • changes in personality
  • loss of initiative
• Provide support for family caregivers:
  • Offer respite care, even if it is for only an hour or two.
  • Encourage friends to stay in touch with caregivers.
  • Organize or help caregivers locate a support group.

chapter six

Hope and Strength Renewed

I (WDH) had known Annette Gillespie for more
than twenty years before I discovered that this quiet mathematician
and devoted Christian was viewed by many in our community as one
of its most valuable health care resources. Scores of people credited
her with helping them overcome some of the most difficult health-related challenges they had faced. I made this discovery following one of
my talks for the local Parkinson's disease support group. I had been
asked to discuss with the group my interest and work in the area of religion and health. At the conclusion of the talk, during the time devoted to refreshments and informal socializing, Dan Levenson, a
member of the group, spoke to me about his wife's struggles with
Parkinson's disease. He first described how devastating the disease
had been. In spite of excellent medical care, it had left her an invalid,
unable to leave their apartment unless she was in a wheelchair. But
then he went on to tell me that something remarkable, something almost miraculous, happened—she began to recover her ability to walk
and engage in other physical activities she had always enjoyed. These
changes, he said, were the result not of a new medication or surgical
procedure, but of a program offered at a local church and led by an
extraordinary woman who also was battling Parkinson's disease.

Just as he was starting to tell me about the program, I noticed a
petite woman walking toward us from across the room, with some
refreshments in her hands. I was quite surprised when Dan pointed to

her and informed me that this was his wife, Doris. Could this really be the woman who only two years ago was in a wheelchair? Here she was, navigating a crowded room by herself, without using a wheelchair or even a walker.

As you can imagine, this story intrigued me. I wanted to find out more about Doris and the program that had been responsible for this remarkable transformation in her life. And I wanted to hear more about the extraordinary woman who had started the program. Fortunately, Doris and Dan were eager to share their story and invited me to visit them at their apartment in a nearby retirement complex.

Entering the Levensons' apartment, I was immediately struck by the paintings and other artwork on the walls. It was an eclectic collection. There were Japanese paintings, etchings of a seaport, a painting of a woman standing along a snowy highway, another of a brightly costumed dancer, and several colorful paintings of wildlife and flowers. Upon closer inspection, I discovered that many of the paintings were signed by Doris. There was one particularly striking painting— of a partially clothed woman standing at the edge of the water gazing out at the horizon. This was also one of Doris's works. In fact, she described it as a self-portrait (although she admits that she gave herself longer legs).

As I went further into their apartment, I found more evidence of her artistic ability. One of the pieces that caught my attention was a framed photograph of Doris in a chapel at the navy base in Guantánamo Bay, Cuba, standing next to some beautiful windows. When I asked about it, she and Dan explained that the windows were ones she designed and made when she lived there years ago. She then showed me a newspaper article about these windows and those in two other chapels at the navy base. Doris had made all of these out of beach glass—fragments of broken bottles and crockery that had washed up on the beach and been worn to a smooth finish by the waves.

I was too busy looking and listening to fully appreciate the effect those moments were having on me, but even then I was aware of being profoundly moved and wanting to know more. I sat down and began asking Doris and Dan about their lives. Both spoke openly about life before and since Doris developed Parkinson's disease, but I was surprised that she didn't seem able to stay seated for long. At first I thought it might be because of her medical condition, but I soon realized that it was simply because there were so many things she wanted to show me. She wanted me to see all the items she had designed and made. She was excited, and her excitement was contagious. She handed me a lovely basket with intricate designs that she had woven out of pine needles. Then she walked across the room to point out some ceramic bookends she had made and painted. I was astonished by the variety of her creative expressions: note cards with her artwork on the front, eggs with beautiful designs painted on them, uniquely crafted earrings, and—one of her most recent projects—a bright, multicolored vest.

As Doris showed me these various items, her brown eyes sparkling all the while, she also told of a fascinating and adventurous life. She had grown up on a wheat farm in Canada, but by the time she completed school, she knew that farming life was not for her. She was ready to move away and to find something else to do. Tired of the cold weather and feeling that her career options would be limited in Canada, she decided to move to the United States—a move she never once regretted. Over the next sixty years she had the opportunity to live in different parts of the country, including California, Missouri, Pennsylvania, Virginia, and now Florida, and to travel to several other countries. Along the way she owned and managed restaurants, became a gourmet cook, and learned to speak both Spanish and Russian. Although she had enjoyed her various work experiences, she welcomed retirement because it gave her more time to explore and develop new interests, including line-dancing, tai chi, and yoga. Doris said that she never tired of searching for new experiences. And wherever she went, whatever she was doing, she was always looking for ways to express through art the things she saw or felt.

My initial sense of awe in the presence of Doris's creative mind was only enhanced when I remembered what had brought us together in the first place: the story of Doris's battle with an incurable, progressive disease. Parkinson's disease is no respecter of persons. Heavyweight champion, Hollywood star, or artist—no one with Parkinson's escapes the inexorable progress of the disease. In Doris, now eighty years old, it had progressed to the point that she was unable to control her body enough to do most of the things she found so gratifying. She still had her artistic eye, but she had lost the ability to take the beautiful images she could see so clearly in her mind and transform them into works of art that could be shared with others. The directions her brain was sending to her arms and hands and fingers were no longer being followed. Sometimes her legs and feet wouldn't move at all when she wanted them to, and other times they insisted on moving when she wanted them to be still.

Doris first realized that something was seriously wrong during one of her yoga classes when she found that she could no longer balance herself on one leg. After several appointments with her family doctor and specialists, she got the diagnosis—Parkinson's disease. In some respects, this was not a surprise. Her father had had Parkinson's disease, as had two of her siblings. She had seen the devastating effects of this condition, especially during a time when there was little medicine could offer. Doris realized that her own life would be altered dramatically and that a very important part of her, her ability to express herself through art, might fade away.

Many of Doris's worst fears came true. In spite of good medical care and the strong support of Dan, this vivacious, independent woman found she could no longer paint, sew, weave, cook, dance, or swim. In fact, by 1999 she could not even leave her apartment to eat in the dining room at the retirement center or visit friends unless Dan was available to take her out in her wheelchair. If it had not been for him, she would have had to move to a nursing home.

Doris's religious faith had helped her during other challenging times, and she knew it would help sustain her through the numerous challenges that would accompany her disease and disability. To nurture her faith, she continued to attend church. Every Sunday, Dan would take her to Westminster Presbyterian Church in DeLand and guide her wheelchair to the front of the sanctuary, where she liked to be seated during the worship service.

Doris found comfort in the prayers and sermons of the pastor, Rev. Ed Hallman, but it was something that his wife, Peggy, said one Sunday that offered Doris not only comfort but hope. She told Doris about one of her neighbors, Annette Gillespie, who also had Parkinson's disease and who had organized a support group that met regularly at a nearby Baptist church. Peggy had seen how much the group had helped Annette, and she had also heard wonderful stories from other participants in the group. She volunteered to get in touch with Annette and to have her send the Levensons information about the next group meeting.

Doris and Dan liked what they learned about the Parkinson's disease support group. The materials they received explained that the group met once a month in the parlor at First Baptist Church. The primary purpose of the meetings was to give individuals with Parkinson's disease and interested family members or friends an opportunity to learn more about it. In addition to hearing guest speakers who could provide the latest information on medical research, treatment options, and community resources, members of the group had the opportunity to discuss their own experiences. They could share both the difficulties they were facing and their successes in meeting various challenges.

The Levensons decided that they wanted to explore becoming a part of this group, so they made plans to attend the next meeting. When the time came, Dan began the lengthy and arduous routine that he had to follow whenever they went to any event in the community. This included taking Doris from their sixth-floor apartment to the car in her wheelchair, helping her into the car, and then loading the wheelchair into the car. Once at the church, Dan had to reverse the routine—unload the wheelchair, help Doris get out of the car and into the chair, and then guide her to the church parlor.

Although attending the support group was a cumbersome, time-consuming, and tiring process, they considered it well worth their effort. It felt good to be among people who were experiencing the same frustrations and challenges. They felt a type of camaraderie that wasn't present in the other groups to which they belonged. And they knew that the information they gained from the guest speakers and during their informal exchanges with other members of the group would be helpful. Also, it was encouraging to hear how many of the individuals in the group managed to continue leading meaningful and rewarding lives in spite of their struggles with Parkinson's disease. The support group's leader, Annette Gillespie, was an outstanding example. Doris and Dan learned that she had been diagnosed with Parkinson's disease almost twenty years earlier but still had managed to lead an active life. In the intervening decades, her life has been busy at work, at home, and in church and the community. At work she taught full-time for the sheer joy of teaching. At home she was a loving wife and mother who commanded the respect of a husband and children who never doubted the accuracy of a neighborhood teenager's characterization of her as the "Rock of Gibraltar."

At church, she gave back much of the energy and caring that had come to her as a youngster from an active church that encouraged her to develop her ability to organize and present complex ideas to an audience. And particularly she gave back the caring spirit that had surrounded her as she developed into young womanhood.

Annette retired a few years early because of the combined assault of Parkinson's and an eye problem she had lived with since she was seventeen and which had become so severe that in the last years of employment she often had to teach mathematics while unable to read the textbook. Since retirement, much of her creative energy has been devoted to helping others who have Parkinson's disease—sometimes through individual counseling in response to an anguished cry for help from a newly diagnosed patient or a caregiver trying to cope with a recalcitrant patient. And always, she focused her energies on the support group the Levensons were exploring.

The Levensons also discovered that many members of the group, including Annette, participated in a special exercise class that met every Thursday at the church. Doris liked the idea of an exercise class designed to accommodate the special needs of people with Parkinson's disease. She had always enjoyed exercise programs, and perhaps this one would help her regain some of the mobility and balance that she had lost. So she and Dan put the class on their calendar for the following Thursday.

When Thursday arrived, Dan and Doris made their way back to the Baptist church. This time they went into the family life center, a multipurpose facility in the building that also houses the chapel and library. There, among banners and musical instruments used in the Sunday contemporary worship service, they found Annette Gillespie, her husband Bryan (who had recently been diagnosed with Parkinson's disease), and a dozen other individuals gathered for the exercise class. Leading the group was Dr. Elizabeth Schumaker, a retired exercise science professor.

Dr. Schumaker—"Liz," the participants called her—took the group through exercises that could be used by each participant, regardless of his or her physical limitations. Some individuals, like Doris, had to do most of the exercises in their seats or have some assistance. In addition to exercises designed to improve strength, balance, and mobility, they practiced strategies and skills they could use should they fall down. Because Parkinson's disease usually impairs balance, many had already fallen and had come to realize that without a strategy for recovery after a fall, they were at the mercy of inexperienced passersby whose efforts to pull them up might cause more damage than the fall itself. The exercise group also learned meditation techniques that help manage stress. And near the end of the hour they stood, joined hands, and danced to a wildly energetic arrangement of "Blue Moon." For some, the music unlocked frozen limbs and offered a few minutes of freedom. For others, the music was a demanding taskmaster, requiring incredible effort to keep up with the patterned movements Liz was calling for as they danced.

Doris felt the class was wonderful. Parts of it had been physically challenging, but she had never been the type to run away from challenges. And Liz and the other participants never let her feel as if she were failing. Instead, they constantly offered words of support and encouragement.

There was no miraculous recovery that day. Doris had to leave the same way she entered—in her wheelchair. But she knew that it was the right program for her. She came away convinced that if she faithfully followed the exercise regimen Dr. Schumaker was teaching them, she could reduce the impact of Parkinson's disease and perhaps even regain some of the physical abilities she had lost.

So Doris decided to add to her weekly routine a second trip to church: Every Sunday she would worship at the Presbyterian church and every Thursday she would exercise at the Baptist church. And on the second Friday of every month she would attend the support group meeting at the Baptist church.

Doris's belief in the healing power of this group proved to be well founded. She got stronger. Gradually her balance and mobility improved, and she regained some control over her arms and hands and fingers. The small but significant gains she saw in herself and others inspired her to work even harder, exercising at home every day. Soon she and Dan were going for walks around the retirement center. The small gains continued and began to add up to large gains. Eventually, Doris, who once had resigned herself to life in a wheelchair, was able to move around unassisted and to go for long walks.

Even more gratifying to Doris was her ability to once again express herself through art. Her artwork took more time now than it had prior to the Parkinson's disease, but at least she could capture in paintings the beauty that she had always been able to see in her mind and share it with others.

What an amazing transformation this was! Doris was again able to leave her apartment by herself and visit with friends throughout the retirement center. She could paint and make gifts for her friends. The life she so loved and valued had been resurrected. And to whom did she owe this amazing transformation?

There was no question in her mind. It was Annette Gillespie. Doris knew that without the support group and exercise class that Annette had started, she would still be in a wheelchair. Like scores of other individuals, Doris was indebted to Annette for adding a healing dimension that went beyond what the doctors could offer.

So, exactly who is Annette Gillespie, the "extraordinary woman" the Levensons talked about—the one responsible for helping Doris regain her ability to walk? How did she become an instrument of healing for so many in her community, and what role did her church play?

Although I had known Annette for more than two decades and was aware that for much of this time she had had Parkinson's disease, I must admit that I had no idea just how much she had meant to others struggling with this disease. I first met Annette and her husband, Bryan, shortly after arriving at Stetson University in 1979. At that time she was teaching in the Department of Mathematics, and Bryan, a professor of English, had an office down the hall from mine. Both went out of their way to help me feel at home as I joined in the life and work of the university. I clearly remember many delightful times I spent with Annette and Bryan during my first few years at Stetson, and I will never forget or fail to appreciate the comfort they gave me as I struggled emotionally with the loss of my parents. For me, both were definitely special people.

I can also remember the first time I noticed Annette having some difficulty moving. It was not unusual for me to see her walking from campus to her nearby home, and she always seemed to move at a comfortable, relaxed pace and to be enjoying her walks. But one day I noticed that her pace had slowed significantly.

The next time I encountered her it appeared that walking had become somewhat of a struggle for her, requiring special effort. (Annette now says that when she tried to walk it was as if hobgoblins had a grip on her feet and she had to pull them away in order to walk.) She was noticing other problems with movement and control of her body: She could not button the sleeve of her blouse, she found getting out of chairs increasingly difficult, and sometimes she had trouble simply putting her body in motion when she wanted to walk across the room.

Annette and Bryan both knew something was wrong, but it wasn't until Annette read a piece of mail that accompanied a solicitation for funds that she realized she had most of the symptoms of Parkinson's disease. A visit to her family doctor and then to a neurologist confirmed what she had suspected.

Although he offered medication that would help her move more easily, she chose to delay starting it because there was some evidence that it would gradually lose its effectiveness. She felt that it would be best to wait until her symptoms were more serious before turning to medication. She was able to do without it for several years, but eventually, as her body responded less and less to her mental commands, she found that she needed the medication.

A couple of years after starting the medication, Annette realized that there might be more she could do to slow the progression of Parkinson's disease, or to at least minimize its impact on her life. As an educator, she was a believer in the importance and power of knowledge. She felt that the more she knew about her disease, the less she would fear it and the better able she would be to cope with it. She also decided that she needed to start a regular exercise routine in order to keep her mobility and balance, and she knew that she needed good instruction and ongoing encouragement to do this.

Annette's search for more knowledge and her determination to exercise on a regular basis led her to explore the possibility of starting a support group for people with Parkinson's disease. She envisioned it as a place where members could learn not only from experts brought in as guest speakers but from each other as well. Those who had only recently been diagnosed with Parkinson's disease could learn what might lie ahead of them—the challenges they would face and the strategies and resources they could use to address them. Their spouses and other family members would have a place where they could come for information and support.

Annette also recognized the potential for the group to help people put into action some of the things they learned about treating Parkinson's disease. She knew that to move from *knowing* to *doing* was not easy for many people, herself included. This was especially true when it came to exercise. It would be much easier for people to adopt and stick with an exercise program if they were part of a group that met regularly.

Annette's idea of starting a support group was enthusiastically embraced by her neurologist. He felt there was a great need for such a group, knowing that patients often wanted more information and emotional support than he could provide during an office visit. He offered to assist Annette by serving as the group's medical adviser, speaking at some of the meetings, and writing to his patients who had Parkinson's disease, encouraging them to join the support group.

Once Annette was convinced of the community's need for a support group and that she could count on the cooperation of key medical professionals, she had to decide where to hold the meetings. What would be the appropriate setting for people to come together to learn more about how to care for themselves and each other? What institution had as part of its mission caring for the mind and spirit as well as the body? The obvious answer was her church, a church that believed caring for the sick was a central part of its ministry. Here was an opportunity for her church to reach out with a new form of ministry to patients and their family members. And for Annette, whose strong sense of altruism was inextricably linked to her deep religious faith, it seemed only natural that a support group should meet at the church.

The church was also where she had developed many of the talents it would take to establish a support group. For example, as a youth she had participated in Baptist Training Union, a Sunday evening program where members were given responsibility for organizing and leading educational programs. More recently, she had taught Sunday school and Bible study classes. Her work in the church had given her plenty of experience locating educational materials, securing speakers for church classes and programs, and putting together a newsletter.

What Annette discovered was that these talents, nurtured and expressed in a religious context, were what were needed to heal. In spite of no formal training in medicine or nursing, Annette became a respected and influential healer. She was able to do what the doctors could not do—help Doris Levenson walk again. Yet the program organized by Annette and offered at the Baptist church was not in opposition to doctors; it was actually in collaboration with them. There was no mysterious, inexplicable miracle here. Rather, individuals such as Doris found renewed hope, strength, and mobility because a dedicated Christian, with the support of her pastor, made a commitment to use her own life experiences to support and guide others as they struggled with their illnesses.

Koenig's Corner

Parkinson's disease is a neurological condition involving irreversible degeneration of cells in a key area of the brain that controls motor activity. Parkinson's is progressive, and spontaneous remissions are extremely rare, with or without exercise. The improvements shown by Doris are truly remarkable and likely result from a combination of social, psychological, physical, and spiritual factors that were at play in her case. Her positive attitude, close relationship with her husband, and involvement in a group of loving and supportive church members undoubtedly had their effects, together with the exercise activity. In Annette's case, because her illness provided an opportunity to help others with similar conditions, her disability was transformed.

Parkinson's Disease—Some Basic Information

- More than 500,000 Americans have Parkinson's disease, with approximately 50,000 new cases diagnosed every year.
- The risk of Parkinson's disease increases with age. The average age of onset is approximately sixty.
- A large proportion—approximately 40 percent—of those who have Parkinson's disease also develop depression.
- There is no known cure for Parkinson's disease.

What Can Be Done in Your Congregation

- Organize, or help members who have Parkinson's disease locate, a support group.
- Organize, or help members who have Parkinson's disease locate, an appropriate exercise program.

chapter seven

Caring for Body, Mind, and Spirit

Anita Parker's visit to the doctor had been heart-breaking. She had learned there that her medical condition was going to require her to give up a part of her life that had been important and meaningful for almost four decades. The medical examination had shown that if she did not do this, the excruciating pain in her back would only get worse and her already restricted range of motion would become even more limited. In fact, her doctor assured her, her physical deterioration would progress to the point that she would require a wheelchair.

What Anita's doctor had insisted that she give up was her special caregiving relationship with her daughter. For the past thirty-six years Anita had devoted almost every day of her life to caring for Stacey, her physically and mentally impaired daughter. Stacey's limitations were so great that there was virtually nothing she could do by herself. These limitations placed tremendous physical demands on Anita. In the mornings, she would have to lift Stacey out of her bed and help her into a wheelchair. Later, when it was time for Stacey's shower, she would need to pick Stacey up out of her wheelchair and lower her onto the shower chair. And whenever Stacey needed to be transferred out of her wheelchair and onto the sofa, Anita again had to lift her. Trips out into the community brought even more challenges.

Stacey's mental and physical limitations also created many emotional struggles for Anita. Since it was hard to find people who were both physically able to lift Stacey and prepared to cope with her limited mental capacity, Anita was seldom able to go out with friends. At an age when most of her friends were free from the daily responsibilities of caring for children, Anita's responsibilities as a caregiver continued with no relief in sight.

Anita's husband, Randy, was also devoted to their daughter and helped care for her whenever he could, but his full-time position as a minister at Cornerstone Church meant that he could not help as much as he would have liked.

In spite of the numerous physical and emotional challenges Stacey presented, Anita cherished her role as Stacey's mother. Theirs was not the typical mother-daughter relationship by any means, but it was still a close, loving relationship. In many respects, they were much closer than most mothers and daughters. And there was something else that made this relationship special. Anita felt that caring for Stacey was her mission in life. It was this mission that gave her life much of its meaning. Anita's loving spirit encompassed the entire family and helped her other children not only learn how to cope with a severely handicapped sibling, but also discover for themselves what Stacey gave them in return. Supported by Anita's love and with her example always before them, they came to share Anita's belief that, for all the difficulties and frustrations Stacey's special needs created, they were fortunate to have Stacey in their family. There was never any doubt among them about Stacey's place in their hearts and in their home.

But what was Anita going to do now that her doctor insisted she no longer engage in any of the physically strenuous aspects of caring for Stacey? She did not question her doctor's diagnosis, and she understood why he insisted that she restrict her physical activities. She knew that this was the right course of action, at least from a strictly physical perspective. Cutting back on many of her caregiving responsibilities would allow her body to heal, or at least prevent it from deteriorating further. But Anita's doctor failed to understand that she did not view her life from a strictly physical perspective. There were other dimensions as well. Drastically reducing her caregiving responsibilities might help her feel better physically, but not emotionally and spiritually. It would represent a major loss for her. She felt it was critical that she remain true to her calling as Stacey's caregiver. What should she do? How could she continue to care for Stacey without damaging her own health?

The answer to Anita's questions appeared in the form of Rita Talbo, a member of the Parkers' church. One day Anita received a phone call from Rita, who asked if she could come by and visit. She said that she had learned of Anita's recent health problems and how they were limiting her ability to care for Stacey. Rita explained that she had experience in home-health nursing and felt that she might be able to help. She also told Anita that she was serving as a volunteer parish nurse for the church and that the assistance she was offering would be a part of this work. Although Anita had not met Rita before and had never heard of a parish nurse, she appreciated the generous offer and invited Rita to visit.

For the next month Rita stopped by once each week to visit with Anita and to help her care for Stacey. One of the most helpful things she did was to assist with giving Stacey her morning shower. Working alongside Anita, Rita had the opportunity to see exactly what was involved in the daily caregiving routine. She also developed a relationship with Anita that allowed them to share with each other their thoughts and feelings about their lives and to join in prayer together. The more Rita watched and listened, the more she understood the dilemma facing Anita. Caring for Stacey, though physically challenging, was a meaningful and gratifying responsibility. Rita could see that it was Anita's vocation, her calling. But certain aspects of it were threatening her health.

Fortunately, Rita saw that there might be a way to resolve Anita's dilemma. As a nurse, Rita had learned how to transfer a patient from a bed to a wheelchair without injuring herself. The key was using proper body mechanics. Rita realized that Anita had never been taught the safe and proper way to transfer Stacey. No doctor or any other professional in the health care system had ever even brought up the subject with her—she had been left on her own. The method

Anita had devised, which involved placing Stacey's hands around her neck, appeared to be what was creating her neck and back problems.

To help correct this problem and to find other ways to relieve some of the physical strain on Anita, Rita called on a physical therapist who also attended Cornerstone Church and who had volunteered to assist with the health ministry. The physical therapist agreed with Rita's assessment, and together they taught Anita a safer way to lift and transfer Stacey. The physical therapist also pointed out that the bed in Stacey's room made transfers more difficult and that obtaining an adjustable hospital bed would facilitate transfers.

Anita was amazed by the beneficial effect these two changes had on her neck and back. She discovered that she could help Stacey out of bed and into her wheelchair without hurting herself, and that other transfers could be accomplished without any pain or injury too. What a marvelous discovery! This meant that she would not have to choose between caring for Stacey and caring for herself. She would be able to continue providing the type of comprehensive care that she loved to give to Stacey.

Anita was overwhelmed with gratitude for the unexpected assistance she had received. The solution to a painful and seemingly impossible dilemma had been found not by her physician or the hospital, but by her church's health ministry team. Rita Talbo, motivated by her faith and equipped with her nursing knowledge, had taken the time to understand the multidimensional nature of Anita's situation. Rita understood that Anita's health consisted of more than being free from disease or pain. For Anita, the emotional and spiritual were as important as the physical.

This is only one example of the creativity and reach of the health ministry at Cornerstone Church. Cornerstone's health ministry can be traced back to 1999, when Rita Talbo approached Pastor Nathan Blackwell. She had been attending the church regularly but was not yet a member. Rita told Pastor Blackwell that she had been deep in prayer for several months seeking God's guidance for her life. A registered nurse with more than twenty years experience in several settings, including the medical-surgical unit of a hospital and a home-health agency, she felt that she was being called to use her nursing skills to establish a ministry of health and healing at Cornerstone Church.

Pastor Blackwell listened carefully as Rita outlined her vision for the church's health ministry. He understood what she wanted to create within the church and could tell that she had both the talents and the motivation to lead this program. He then asked what she needed to initiate such a ministry. Rita said that she felt an important first step would be to obtain training in parish nursing. She explained that this relatively new specialization in nursing prepared registered nurses to serve in several roles in their congregations—health educator, personal health counselor, referral agent, coordinator of volunteers, developer of support groups, integrator of faith and health, and health advocate. Pastor Blackwell's response was not only to encourage her to pursue this training, but also to offer to have the church pay for her tuition and the other expenses she would incur during her training.

Rita's training as a parish nurse was supplemented by her participation in one of the Lay Health Educator training programs offered by Florida Hospital. Although her nursing background had given her ample medical knowledge, these workshops provided her with many new ideas about how to apply her medical knowledge and skills within a congregation. She also learned more about the various resources in the community, and she was able to establish a good working relationship with the hospital staff that would allow her to call on them for assistance as she developed her health ministry at Cornerstone Church.

Once Rita had completed her training, Pastor Blackwell asked that she introduce the concept of parish nursing to the congregation during the Sunday worship services. To do this, he suggested that she work with members of the church's drama team to write a fifteen-minute skit that could illustrate some of the key elements of parish nursing. Rita was excited about the idea of reaching so many members of the congregation so quickly, but she was not exactly thrilled to have to get up in front of such a large group. In fact, it made her nervous just to think about it. She was much more comfortable working on a one-to-one basis. Still, she knew that this was an important opportunity to teach the congregation about parish nursing and that she should not let her anxiety get in the way. Fortunately, when the time for the skit came, Pastor Blackwell's good sense of humor helped Rita relax enough to get through it with no difficulties, and the reaction of the congregation was warm and encouraging.

The first health program Rita offered was blood-pressure checks once a month immediately after the worship service. This is often where parish nurses start their work, and it was a good way for members to get to know Rita and to learn more about parish nursing. And, of course, it also allowed Rita to give them feedback about their health and to talk with them about the risks associated with high blood pressure.

Rita knew from her parish nurse training and from conversations with other parish nurses that frequently they were not able to offer many congregational health programs aside from the blood-pressure checks and counseling for parishioners who needed to talk to someone about a medical issue. But Rita was determined to do more. She felt that she needed to take the initiative to reach out to members of the congregation and the community. She wanted to adopt a proactive approach, encouraging people to take steps that would prevent illnesses and injuries.

Fortunately, Rita's pastor understood and supported her plans for an innovative and comprehensive approach. He liked her ideas about the health ministry and how it could tie in with other church ministries. Firmly believing that one of his major responsibilities as a pastor was to help members develop their gifts, he encouraged her to move ahead with her plans.

Rita decided that one of the first subjects she needed to address was breast cancer, the second-most common type of cancer among American women (skin cancer is the most common). She knew that it was important to impress upon women the need for early detection and to give them the knowledge and skills they needed to accomplish it. She also wanted to give hope to women who had been diagnosed with breast cancer or other cancers. They needed to realize that a diagnosis of cancer was not a death sentence.

Instead of simply handing out brochures on breast cancer, Rita organized a mother-daughter tea held in the dining room at the church. She invited the women of the church to attend and encouraged them to bring their mother or daughter. At the tea a representative of the American Cancer Society handed out some of their materials and spoke on two of the organization's programs: Triple Touch and Reach to Recovery. The Triple Touch program emphasizes early detection through regular self-examinations, annual clinical examinations, and mammography screening, while the Reach to Recovery program helps women cope with their breast cancer experience by having a specially trained volunteer (a breast cancer survivor) reach out to them and offer support and hope. Rita also arranged to have small gifts for each of the women who attended, and a massage therapist donated her time to give the women brief massages. These added features reflected Rita's belief that women who were facing the threat or actual experience of breast cancer deserved a little pampering.

One of the women who attended the mother-daughter tea was Dodie Corneile. Dodie was already in the middle of an intense battle with breast cancer. She had been diagnosed with an aggressive form that required her doctors to use all the weapons in their arsenal. These included surgery (a double mastectomy), radiation, and high-dose chemotherapy. The treatments had left her with little energy and no hair, but Dodie felt it was important to attend this event and to bring both her mother, also a breast cancer survivor, and her daughter.

For Dodie, the fact that this breast cancer program was being held at a church had special significance. One of the most difficult challenges she had faced as she endured the chemotherapy was isolation. With the powerful drugs weakening her immune system, she was forced to stay home by herself most of the time. She was comforted by her faith and felt God's presence during this period, but she also found that there were times she wanted to have someone "with skin" sitting in the room with her. She wanted to be able to reach out and touch someone.

This is where the church proved to be so valuable to Dodie. Several women from the church, upon learning of her condition, offered to come by on a regular basis. These women brought her meals, sat with her, listened to her, prayed with her, and hugged her. They gave her the support she needed to fight off her most dangerous enemy—despair.

Knowing how important the church could be in the fight against breast cancer and the despair that can accompany it, Dodie wanted to be a part of the first mother-daughter tea. And she was not disappointed with what she found there. The food was good, the massage felt wonderful, and the information offered by the representative from the American Cancer Society was helpful. But there was something else. A warm, loving feeling permeated the event. There was an emotional bonding with the other women that gave her more hope and a greater sense of support. She left with her strength enhanced and her spirit renewed.

Dodie also came away with a sense of mission. She felt called to put her faith into action by helping Rita with her health ministry. Dodie knew there must be more women in the congregation and the surrounding community who needed to learn about breast cancer, and certainly there were women going through treatment for breast cancer who felt isolated and in need of support. She felt that her experience would enable her to be of help to both groups. Dodie also wanted to see the church reach out to men on the subject of breast cancer, because she felt that men could play an important role by encouraging their wives to participate in early detection programs. She also realized that men often aren't equipped to handle many of the emotional issues they face when they discover that their wife has breast cancer, and she wanted the church to offer men the guidance and support they needed.

The success of the mother-daughter tea inspired Rita to develop a program on cancer she could offer the men of the church. For the men, instead of a "tea time" at the church, she would offer a father-son "tee time" at a nearby golf course. The men could play a round of golf, have a nice lunch, and then hear a brief program on the importance of early detection of prostate cancer.

This type of creative programming caught the attention of more and more members of the church. They began to understand what it meant to have a parish nurse in their congregation. They realized that there was someone to whom they could turn when they needed information about health care resources or if they had concerns about a treatment recommendation. And she could offer more than information. She would pray with them and care for their spiritual needs as well.

One woman in the congregation asked to talk to Rita about her doctor's recommendation that she have surgery to remove a tumor. She knew she should have the surgery, but she was so fearful of the hospital and what the surgery would involve that she could not bring herself to schedule the operation. Rita understood her fears and took the time to explain what the surgery could accomplish and what it would be like to go through the surgery. They discussed preop and postop procedures and how the anesthesia was likely to affect her. This was exactly what the woman needed to know. The information and support she received from Rita helped her overcome her fears and gave her confidence that she could handle the surgery.

On several occasions, requests for assistance came from people outside the congregation. For example, one day Rita received a call from a woman in California. She was facing a problem that more and more people face every year—they live thousands of miles from their elderly parents. In her case, her elderly mother lived by herself near Cornerstone Church. Her mother's health had deteriorated to the point that she needed some assistance at home, but the daughter did not know what was available in the community. How could she find out about community resources? Fortunately, one of her mother's friends suggested that she contact Cornerstone Church, because it was known in the community for its health ministry.

This was the type of request for assistance that Rita was well prepared to handle. Since she felt that an important part of her ministry was serving as the bridge between people in need and the appropriate health care resources, she had made it a point to stay informed about the various agencies and professionals in the community. After talking to the woman enough to get a sense of her mother's medical problems and limitations, she was able to make several helpful recommendations and to get her linked up with the Council on Aging and its Meals on Wheels program. Rita also helped the woman think about other health-related issues that she and her mother could be facing soon. One suggestion Rita offered was that the time had come for the daughter to talk to her mother about advance directives. They needed to discuss what type of end-of-life care she would want and then prepare advance directives that would ensure that her wishes would be honored. Having all of this arranged before an acute health event disrupted her mother's life would help avoid unnecessary, expensive, and unwanted medical interventions while ensuring that appropriate, desired health care is received.

As more requests for information and advice on medical matters came in, Rita decided to make it easier for people to reach her. She did this by setting aside five hours every Wednesday when she would be available at the church to talk with anyone who had questions or concerns about health issues. They could either contact her by telephone or stop by the church to see her.

Rita also began thinking of more ways she and the health ministry team could reach out to the congregation, even the youngest among them. Among the programs they developed were:

- New moms visitation. Members of the health ministry team visit first-time mothers in their homes and offer them information on basic health topics and the church's day care services.
- Baby-sitting classes. Aware that much of the child care in the church nursery and in homes in the community is provided by teenage baby-sitters, the health ministry team helps protect these young children by offering teenagers from the church and the community classes on how to care for infants and young children.

- First aid and CPR classes. A member of the health ministry team who is a certified Red Cross instructor offers training in first aid and cardiopulmonary resuscitation.
- Nutrition and exercise classes. The health ministry team educates members about lifestyle changes they can make to prevent disease and to enhance their health, and supports their efforts to make these changes.
- An influenza vaccination clinic. The health ministry team arranges for influenza vaccinations to be offered at the church every fall, just before flu season.
- Vascular screening. Once each year the health ministry team arranges for vascular screening to be offered at the church.
- A health fair. The health ministry team holds a health fair at the church each year to help raise awareness of various health issues and provide attendees with information about resources.
- A newsletter. Rita edits a monthly newsletter on health and wellness that is distributed to members of the congregation.
- A bulletin board. The health ministry team maintains an educational bulletin board where information about national monthly observances and health-related community events are posted.

Cornerstone Church presents an inspiring story. In less than four years, this church in a rapidly growing community near Orlando has established a remarkable health ministry that reaches throughout the congregation, into the community, and sometimes even across the country. Again, the inspiration came from a single individual who felt God's call to share her professional life experiences with her faith community. And the implementation occurred because of the insightful response of a pastor who recognized that an important part of his own calling was to encourage laypersons to share the task of ministering.

Although Rita Talbo and Pastor Blackwell would be quick to say that they did not have all the answers, their experience involved six elements that any congregation might do well to consider as it seeks to fulfill its varied roles as a church:

- Recognition of a need
- Volunteering of service
- Acceptance of and commitment to the ministry
- Vision of a comprehensive plan
- Specific preparation for the task
- Orientation and initiation by way of simple programs that can lead into the expanded vision

Koenig's Corner

Almost every middle- to large-sized congregation has either current or retired health professionals who have the ability to help initiate a health ministry as Rita did. Identifying these people, inspiring them to get involved, and organizing them can achieve significant physical and spiritual health benefits for the congregation. As church members become involved in maintaining their own health and ensuring that the health needs of other members are met, they feel a greater sense of purpose, commitment, and belonging. It does, indeed, take a village to care for the sick among us—and each member of a faith community has talents and abilities to share. If these talents are buried, then both that individual's health and the health of the faith community will suffer. When these talents are identified and mobilized, everyone benefits.

Breast Cancer—Some Basic Information

- More than 200,000 women are diagnosed with breast cancer each year, making it the second-most common cancer among women.
- The risk of breast cancer increases with age.
- The risk of breast cancer is greater among women who have a history of the cancer in their family.

- Although European American women are slightly more likely than African American women to develop breast cancer, African American women are more likely to die from breast cancer, because their cancers are often diagnosed later and are thus harder to treat.

What Can Be Done in Your Congregation

- Provide members with the American Cancer Society's guidelines for the early detection of breast cancer:
  - Women age forty and older should have a screening mammogram and a clinical breast exam by a health care professional every year.
  - Women between the ages of twenty and thirty-nine should have a clinical breast examination by a health professional every three years.
  - Women age twenty or older should perform a breast self-examination every month.
- Sponsor a program on breast cancer for women of the church. Guest speakers could include an oncologist, nurse, representative of the American Cancer Society, or breast cancer survivor.

Prostate Cancer—Some Basic Information

- More than 200,000 men are diagnosed with prostate cancer every year, making it the second-most common type of cancer among men.
- Prostate cancer is most common in men over the age of fifty.
- The rate of prostate cancer in African American men is approximately 70 percent greater than that found in European American men.

What Can Be Done in Your Congregation

- Encourage men to follow the American Cancer Society's guidelines:
  - Beginning at age fifty, all men who have at least a ten-year life expectancy should have both a Prostate Specific Antigen (PSA) blood test and a digital rectal exam annually.
  - Men in high-risk groups—African Americans, men with close family members who have had prostate cancer—should begin testing at age forty-five.
- Sponsor a program on prostate cancer for men of the church. Guest speakers could include a urologist, a representative of the American Cancer Society, or a prostate cancer survivor.

chapter eight

Reaching the Multitudes

The Sunday worship services at Pabellón de la
Victoria, a Spanish-speaking church on the outskirts of Orlando, are
joyous gatherings. Worshipers can feel the enthusiasm and friendliness of the congregation the moment they enter the brightly lit sanctuary. Ushers, in their burgundy blazers, greet each person with a
smile and a warm handshake or hug. As people move to their seats,
they frequently stop to embrace friends. Everyone, including young
children, teenagers, and adults of all ages, seems to be excited about
being at the service. Even visitors who have only a limited understanding of the Spanish language feel welcome and comfortable
among their fellow worshipers.

The enthusiasm of the congregation increases as the music begins.
A praise band that includes musicians on piano, electric keyboard,
guitars, drums, tambourine, and trumpet accompanies the choir and
soloists. On many hymns the congregation joins in, singing, clapping,
and shouting. Many worshipers raise their hands as they sing. Even
the small babies seem to enjoy this part of the service, as they sway
back and forth in their parents' arms.

The praise band and choir are then joined by a group of girls in
white dresses and colorful aprons who begin to worship through
dance. They seem to move effortlessly, gliding back and forth across
the front of the sanctuary, their graceful movements enhanced by the
brightly colored scarves and ribbons they wave through the air.

After a half hour of music and dance, Dr. Ruben Perez, pastor of Pabellón de la Victoria, steps to the pulpit to welcome people and give announcements. But he doesn't remain in the pulpit long. Soon he is out in the congregation, walking down the aisle and warmly greeting both members and visitors.

Returning to the pulpit, Dr. Perez leads the congregation through the Scripture lessons and prayer. He then begins his sermon. Preaching with great energy and conviction, Dr. Perez has no difficulty holding the attention of the congregation. They listen closely to his words, often responding with cries of "Amen."

Visitors are likely to assume that Dr. Perez will focus solely on spiritual matters in his sermon. But for Dr. Perez and the members of this evangelical, charismatic church, the physical dimension of life is also important. Dr. Perez frequently reminds worshipers that it should not be overlooked. He preaches that Christians need to be concerned about their physical health as well as their spiritual health. They cannot serve and glorify God to the fullest extent of their abilities unless they care properly for their bodies. Furthermore, Dr. Perez feels the church should assume a major role in helping its members meet these responsibilities.

When Dr. Perez talks to his congregation about the importance of Christians caring for their bodies and offers them advice about the steps they should take to maintain their health, he speaks with greater authority than most pastors, because he is also a practicing physician. His training in internal and family medicine and years of practice have given him an understanding of not only diseases, but also the human shortcomings that often allow diseases to go undetected and untreated.

He knows that too often people are not aware that they have a potentially harmful medical condition. Sometimes they ignore or misinterpret symptoms and thus fail to get an accurate diagnosis and the appropriate treatment. They may assume that certain symptoms don't require any more than over-the-counter medications they can pick up at their drugstore. And he knows that many people assume that as long as they are not experiencing any pain or discomfort, they must be healthy. They are not aware that they could have a condition that might cripple or kill and yet not have any symptoms. They don't think about the possibility of having high blood pressure or diabetes or glaucoma, or they fail to realize the great harm that can come from any of these diseases.

Dr. Perez is also keenly aware that members of minority communities often have difficulty obtaining medical services. For some, the lack of money or health insurance serves as a barrier to good health care. For others, language or cultural differences may be the obstacles. Dr. Perez believes that the church can and should find ways to help people overcome these problems and obtain the health care they need.

To address these needs, Dr. Perez has led his congregation in establishing a health ministry that regularly educates members about important health matters and brings medical services to them at the church. An excellent example of this ministry is a program they held on Helicobacter pylori (H. pylori), a bacterium that is found in the stomach and that causes more than 90 percent of duodenal ulcers and almost 80 percent of gastric ulcers. People infected with H. pylori also have an increased risk of developing gastric cancer. Another fact, especially important for the members of Pabellón de la Victoria, is that H. pylori is more prevalent among Hispanics. This is the disturbing, but largely unknown, information that Dr. Perez shared with his congregation. But he also brought them good news. H. pylori, once detected, is easy to treat, with therapy consisting of ten days to two weeks of an appropriate antibiotic.

To help members determine whether they were infected with H. pylori and needed treatment, the church arranged for Florida Hospital to sponsor a screening that was held in church facilities immediately after the Sunday worship service. Dr. Perez announced the screening during the service and encouraged all who had been experiencing any pain or discomfort in or around their stomach to participate. Many in the congregation took advantage of this program, and Dr. Perez later learned that at least one person had definitely benefited from this screening. A few weeks after the program, a woman in the congregation spoke to him and thanked him for teaching them about H. pylori and arranging the screening. She explained that she had been experiencing abdominal pain for a long time but had never done anything more than try to control the symptoms with over-the-counter medication. Through the screening she learned that she was positive for H. pylori. Armed with this information and the knowledge of how it should be treated, she saw her physician, obtained the medication she needed, and was now symptom free.

As gratifying as it was to hear of stories like this from a member of the church, Dr. Perez and his congregation were not content to have a health ministry that benefited only church members. They felt called to reach out to residents in the surrounding neighborhoods and to make a special effort to contact members of the large Hispanic community in central Florida, a rapidly growing group that represented 17 percent of the population in this region.

The congregation decided that the first step they should take in an effort to extend their health ministry into the community was to organize a health fair. Their plan for the fair was to offer information on a wide range of health topics and to provide free screenings that could detect health threats early. Since they were particularly interested in reaching the Hispanic community, they decided to have music and food that would appeal to Hispanics. And since they wanted this to be a festive event that would attract families and individuals of all ages, they also decided to have games and rides that would appeal to children. It would be held on church grounds on a Sunday afternoon in the fall, a time of year when the mild temperatures are ideal for outdoor gatherings.

As they developed their plans further, they realized that the health fair they were envisioning would be a large undertaking, even for a congregation of five hundred. They knew they would need the assistance of other organizations and health care providers in order to have the range of services they wanted to offer. They asked Florida Hospital for its support, and the hospital generously offered to help sponsor the fair and provide the personnel and equipment needed to handle the screenings for blood pressure, cholesterol, and diabetes.

The planning committee also arranged for the county health department to send some of its staff, along with educational materials on HIV/AIDS and other sexually transmitted diseases. Next came various health professionals. An ophthalmologist offered to do screenings for glaucoma. An audiologist volunteered to perform hearing tests, and an optometrist agreed to conduct vision tests. Several health care companies offered to donate educational materials on various topics, including depression, anxiety, high blood pressure, heart disease, and diabetes.

Once Dr. Perez and his congregation had succeeded in enlisting the support and cooperation of numerous organizations and professionals, they had to turn their attention to publicizing the event. The health services and materials they had pulled together would be of little value unless they could attract a large audience. Flyers and word of mouth could be used to publicize the event in the nearby neighborhoods, but they also wanted to reach members of the Hispanic community who lived in other parts of the metropolitan Orlando area. To do this, they turned to radio. Here they had an advantage. Dr. Perez, who already had a regular call-in show on a popular Spanish-speaking radio station, used part of his time on the air to talk about the health fair.

The big day finally arrived, and it was a beautiful day—not a cloud in the sky. Banners announcing the health fair hung from the church building and the large tent that had been erected on a grassy lot next to the church. Dozens of tables were set up under the tent. Seated at some of the tables were nurses and other health professionals, ready to conduct screenings and offer advice. At other tables were displays of educational materials. And at still others were pens, pencils, key chains, notepads, and other items—inexpensive but useful gifts that would serve as a reminder of what had been learned at the fair and that would, perhaps, provide an important address and telephone number of an organization waiting to help. Under the church portico a stage and sound system had been set up for the musical groups that would be performing.

Smaller tents also had been erected on the grounds. These were for the food that had been donated and cooked by members of the congregation. And for the children, there were balloons, a basketball court, games, and rides.

The time had finally come to discover whether their extensive planning and hard work would pay off. Would the fair attract a large crowd? Would people who had no connection to the church stop by? Would they be successful in reaching a large number from the Hispanic community? Answers came quickly, and for each question the response was a resounding "Yes!" Scanning the license plates of the cars that came streaming into the parking lot, those who had worked so hard preparing for this day could see that many cars bore tags from surrounding counties. It wasn't long before the lot was full—as were the hearts of the parishioners—and people who had driven some distance to take advantage of this remarkable opportunity had to find parking spaces along the adjoining streets.

Soon there were lines at the tables. It was clear that people were at the fair for more than food and entertainment. They were definitely interested in obtaining information on health matters, and particularly on their own health. They lined up to have their blood pressure checked and to see if their blood sugar or cholesterol levels were high and, if so, what they should do about it. They picked up informational brochures and inquired about various topics. They wanted to know about services that were available in the community. And when they had questions, they were pleased to discover that there was no language barrier to overcome: There were plenty of health professionals present who spoke Spanish.

People continued coming to the fair throughout the afternoon, and the lines at the tables remained until the very end. Representatives from the hospital and other health organizations were delighted that so many were interested in their services and information, and everyone involved in planning and working at the fair was surprised to learn that by the end of the day more than 5,000 people had attended.

It was an amazing accomplishment for this congregation of 500. They had extended the healing ministry of Christ to 5,000 people, and they were elated. They knew that they had done more than screen the masses; they had also been channels of God's love to 5,000 individuals. And from the reports of the health professionals conducting the screenings and the comments of those who attended, church members knew the health fair had, in some cases, touched some of these individual lives with potentially life-saving information. There were those who had discovered that in spite of feeling healthy, they might have a serious medical condition and that they needed to obtain further medical testing and care. Some of those attending learned for the first time the steps they needed to take to reduce their risk of developing diabetes or heart disease. And others learned how to recognize and respond to depression.

For Dr. Perez and the members of Pabellón de la Victoria, the tremendous success of the health fair was a clear sign that they had identified an important need in the community and an effective way to respond to this need. People were hungry for information on health and medical care, and they were especially eager to obtain this information from individuals who understood their culture and language. Strengthened by what they witnessed at their health fair, the members of Pabellón de la Victoria are committed to continuing their ministry of health and healing, and they hope they will soon be able to extend their reach even further by adding a parish nurse to the church staff. If their past is any indicator of their future, there can be little doubt that commitment and hard work will again reap handsome rewards: Large numbers of people will be helped to achieve and maintain a healthful lifestyle, and they will know also that someone cares for them.

Koenig's Corner

Minority communities often experience the worst health care and have health conditions diagnosed at advanced stages, when they are difficult to treat and require expensive emergency-room care or acute hospitalization. Getting access to disease screening and preventive health care is a real problem for many African Americans, Hispanics, Cambodians, Middle Easterners, and other ethnic minorities. The one place where members of all ages from these communities typically congregate is the church, temple, or mosque. Because children, adults, and seniors all come together to worship on a regular basis in these settings, they are ideal for reaching those people who cannot afford regular health care or for whom language barriers limit access. Furthermore, since one or both adults in many minority families must work long hours to support their families, often there is not time to go to physicians or health clinics. Having these programs in churches makes health care convenient. More significant, when a minister emphasizes the importance of health, people listen. A minister often serves not only as a religious leader, but as an influential community leader as well. As such, clergy can have a real impact on the health of the membership. This makes particularly good sense given the emphasis placed on health and healing in Christianity, and, to some extent, in other religious traditions as well. Most ministers would rather lead a healthy congregation than to have to expend large amounts of time and resources caring for a membership that is sick, chronically ill, or emotionally distressed. Thus, minority churches are now often leading the way to form partnerships with local hospitals to help maintain the health of their membership and broader ethnic communities, and it is the minority clergy who are often advocating, mobilizing, and taking the lead to make this possible.

Glaucoma—Some Basic Information

- Two to three million Americans have glaucoma.
- Because there are no symptoms in the early stages of glaucoma, as many as half of these people are not aware they have the condition.
- Glaucoma is the second-leading cause of adult blindness.
- If glaucoma is detected and treated in time, blindness can be prevented.
- There are several effective treatments for glaucoma, including medications, laser surgery, and conventional surgery.
- African Americans are four to five times more likely than European Americans to have glaucoma.

- Individuals who are diabetic are also at increased risk of having glaucoma, as are those with a family history of the condition.
- The National Eye Institute recommends that African Americans over the age of forty and everyone else over the age of sixty have a comprehensive eye examination every two years to check for glaucoma.

What Can Be Done in Your Congregation

- Distribute information about glaucoma. Be sure to emphasize the large number of individuals who are not aware that they have glaucoma and the risk of blindness if it is not detected and treated.
- Sponsor a talk by an ophthalmologist or optometrist and arrange for screenings to accompany the presentation.
- Encourage individuals in high-risk groups to have comprehensive eye examinations—through dilated pupils—every two years.

chapter nine

Out of the Darkness
and into the Light

Karen had been trapped in a painful and at times
frightening depression for almost a year. The 36-year-old office manager and mother of three continued to attend church during most of
this time, but only because the other members of her family insisted
she do so. Had it not been for them, she would have stayed in bed on
Sunday mornings with the sheet pulled over her head, trying to block
out what seemed to be a cold and hostile world. She didn't feel like
seeing her friends at church. They all looked so happy and enthusiastic. And she no longer found the worship service a joyous or meaningful experience. It felt like a lie to sing any of the inspirational
hymns, and she could not concentrate on the sermon for more than a
few moments. Church had become just one more setting where she
felt uncomfortable and out of place.

But it was at church one Sunday that she discovered a tiny sliver of
hope. It came in the form of a brochure tacked to one of the bulletin
boards. The brochure announced a Congregational Health Ministries
Conference for Clergy and Laity that would be held in a few weeks at
a nearby church. The topic for the conference was *Recognizing and
Responding to Depression.* Next to the brochure was a letter from Rev.
Paul Juvinall, a minister at First United Methodist Church of Orlando
and a member of the conference advisory council, encouraging his
fellow Methodists to attend this program.

Several of the topics listed on the announcement spoke to Karen
and seemed to offer a ray of light. One of the talks, "Though I Walk
through the Valley: A Personal Account of Depression," was going to
be given by a local minister. The title of another talk, "Depression: The
Darkness and the Light," suggested there might be hope for someone
suffering from depression. So did one titled "The Good News: Effective Treatments for Depression." And the fact that it would be held at
a church and was aimed expressly at people of faith gave it special appeal. Throughout most of her life, Karen had relied on her faith and
her church during tough times. But she had not been able to reach out
and ask for help during her depression. And, like many who are depressed, she managed to keep her pain and suffering from others.

There might have been a few members of Karen's church who realized she had changed somewhat in the past year, but most who saw
her on Sundays probably did not notice any changes. To them, she appeared to be much the same person she had been since moving to
town and joining the church more than a decade earlier, and they
most probably assumed that she was doing fine. Perhaps she was a little busier now and had less time to participate in church programs,
but there did not seem to be any reason to be especially concerned
about her.

Even those who did notice some changes in her appearance and
the degree of her involvement in church activities did not seem to be
aware of what Karen was actually feeling. When it looked as if Karen
had not had a good night's sleep, they generally assumed it was because she had been up late the night before taking care of a sick
child. If she did not come to Bible study regularly, they thought it
might be because of extra work at the office. When she seemed qui-
eter than normal during group discussions, they assumed she was
tired or distracted. And Karen didn't say anything that would help
them understand what she was going through. She was embarrassed,
even ashamed, at some of her thoughts and feelings. She felt that she
had changed in some very fundamental ways, and she did not like
the person she had become. Making this even worse was the fact that
she could not see how she would ever be able to change back into a

person she liked. She felt completely hopeless and helpless about her situation.

Karen also avoided saying anything to her pastor about her despair. There were several reasons she didn't want him to know anything about it. She doubted that he could even understand what she was experiencing. He always seemed so positive about life. And Karen feared that he might view her depression as a consequence of her faith not being strong enough. She often thought that herself. Even if he did not doubt her faith, she still did not want him to know how she had changed. She wanted him to think well of her, and she was certain that it would be impossible for him to do so if he knew some of the things she was thinking and feeling. So Karen went through this painful and difficult period of her life without the help and support of her pastor or her friends from the church.

What was life like for Karen during this time? Looking back, Karen describes it as a dark time during which she alternated between periods of great pain and periods when she felt nothing. There were days when she did not even feel alive inside—the best she could do was to force herself to go through the motions of daily life, just "faking it." And this only made her feel worse, like a fraud, pretending to be someone she really was not. There were many nights when Karen could not think of a reason to go on living. And often death seemed like a good alternative. At least she would be free of the pain.

Karen dreaded the start of every day. Since she could get no more than a few hours of sleep, even if she went to bed early in the evening, she never felt like getting up when the alarm sounded. And, in spite of the fact that she had lost more than ten pounds, her body felt heavier than normal as she dragged it out of bed. She admitted that there were many mornings she would not have been able to force herself to get out of bed if it had not been for her responsibilities as a mother. She knew that the children depended on her to prepare their breakfasts and get them to school.

Karen was particularly disturbed that her feelings about her children had changed dramatically. She still loved them as much as ever, but she found that she no longer enjoyed them. The lively, joyous feelings that had almost always been present when she was with them were missing now. Their hugs and smiles and giggles had no impact on her emotions. A request to join them for a bike ride seemed like an unreasonable demand since it would inevitably drain her of the little energy she might have. She had trouble staying focused on their words as they gave their enthusiastic reports of the day's activities and accomplishments. And even worse, Karen thought she had detected a change in her children's feelings about her. She was afraid they had been able to see that she could not enjoy them the way she had before. And this made Karen feel like an absolute failure as a mother.

Karen's feelings—or, rather, absence of feelings—for her husband were also disturbing. It wasn't that she was unhappy with her marriage or husband; in fact, she felt extremely lucky to be married to him. But she often felt guilty about the relationship. She had so little to offer him. There were times when she thought that a divorce would be the best thing for him. Why would he want to stay with her? She could no longer offer him the warmth and affection she had given so freely before. She desperately wanted to, but where would it come from? There wasn't any warmth or life inside her. Her body was unresponsive to his touch, and she knew he could sense the change. Even their special evenings together that they had always enjoyed, times they would get a baby-sitter for the children and go out to dinner and a movie by themselves, no longer seemed special. They brought her no pleasure, and it took such tremendous energy to pretend that she was enjoying the time with him.

Her depression affected her work as well. She no longer found her job enjoyable or even manageable. The workload seemed overwhelming, and she had trouble keeping her mind on the tasks at hand. Previously always thorough and meticulous in her work, she was now making careless mistakes.

The negative thoughts that constantly rolled over and over in her mind also kept her from enjoying reading her favorite books. She found it impossible to read more than a few paragraphs at a time, and even then she had trouble remembering what she had just read.

And so, in spite of a loving husband and children, a good job, supportive coworkers, and a caring church family, Karen felt alone, worthless, and hopeless. There seemed no way out of this deep, dark depression. She had no idea which way to turn, where to look for help, until she read the brochure about the health ministries conference on depression. Maybe, just maybe, she would find some answers there.

Two weeks later, when she attended the conference, Karen did find some answers, along with some surprises. The first surprise of the day was the number of people interested in the topic of depression. When Karen arrived at College Park Baptist Church, she discovered that more than two hundred people had registered for the conference. This was far more than she had ever imagined. And they came from various faiths and denominations.

The second surprise, something she heard during a lunchtime conversation with one of the members of College Park Baptist Church, was that the church had volunteered to host the conference on depression because of its commitment to establish a health ministry that would serve members of the community as well as the members of the church. This health ministry had started in 1995 when Dr. Charles Horton, the senior pastor at College Park Baptist, had learned of a new program being offered to religious congregations by Florida Hospital, a large medical center just a couple of miles from the church. The purpose of this program was to train members of congregations to coordinate health programs. Dr. Horton immediately liked this idea because he believed that church members can be highly effective ministers, and that it was his responsibility to help them identify and develop their gifts.

After careful consideration, Dr. Horton approached Barbara Pearson and asked if she would be interested in participating in a hospital-based Lay Health Educators training program that would prepare her to organize a health ministry at College Park Baptist. Barbara was already involved in many different areas of church life at College Park Baptist. A schoolteacher by training, she enjoyed teaching Sunday school classes, and, with her lovely soprano voice, she was a valued member of the choir. She also took on many informal responsibilities, such as making sure that anyone new to the congregation was warmly greeted each Sunday. Knowing Barbara's heart and many talents, Dr. Horton felt that she was the right person to head up this new ministry.

Uncertain at first about how she could ever lead a ministry of health and healing, Barbara soon "caught the vision." She quickly became aware of people's hunger for more information and support when confronted by medical issues. People knew that they needed to learn more about preventing diseases and injuries. They knew that they needed more information about managing their own chronic conditions and supporting others when the burdens of illness threatened to overwhelm them. With the tools she had been given in the Lay Health Educator program at Florida Hospital, Barbara set out to meet many of these needs.

Dr. Horton worked closely with Barbara to develop a health ministry that would reach throughout the congregation and into the community. He gave the new program an initial push in January 1996 by preaching a sermon on the topic "A Theology of Health" in which he called on members of the congregation to be good stewards of one of God's greatest creations—their bodies. He told of his own commitment to pay greater attention to his health and asked that his parishioners do the same. "I am asking you to take charge of your personal health. Visualize your body as precious in God's sight." One way they could do this would be to take advantage of a series of programs on health issues that Barbara had organized. Through these seminars they could learn how to care for themselves and for each other.

This ministry of health and healing, initially built around Wednesday-evening workshops led by physicians, pharmacists, nurses, psychologists, and other health professionals, became a vital part of the overall ministry of College Park Baptist Church. Members of the congregation and residents of the surrounding community were able to learn about a number of important health issues, including orthopedics, heart disease, cancer, medications, diabetes, nutrition, alcoholism and substance abuse, Alzheimer's disease, and eating disorders.

Now, three years after initiating the program, Dr. Horton, Barbara Pearson, and many other members of the church were ready and eager to work with hospital officials, university professors, psychiatrists, and psychologists to extend their health ministry even further into the community. They wanted to help leaders from other congregations learn how they could recognize and respond to members of their congregation who were depressed. And they wanted to offer hope and direction to individuals who were suffering from this condition and did not know where to turn.

Karen had no trouble listening to the speakers that day. She felt that each one was talking directly to her. When the first speaker, Dr. Peter Rabins, a noted psychiatrist from the Johns Hopkins University School of Medicine, described the symptoms of depression, she found she could relate to each one. Oddly, this was reassuring. It gave her a sense of relief that what she had been experiencing for a year had a name and was recognized by the medical profession as a serious condition. Even more reassuring was the encouraging news about treatments. She learned that there were several effective treatment options, including antidepressant medications and psychotherapy.

Dr. Rabins was followed by Dr. Richard Myer, the pastor at First Presbyterian Church of Maitland. It was his presentation that meant so much to Karen. This was the first time she had ever heard a minister talk about his own struggles with depression, a depression so severe that during an earlier pastorate he had to ask his congregation for an extended leave of absence. Dr. Myer was relieved when the church granted his request, but relief soon turned to anxiety as he thought about the possibility that they might not want to take him back, even if he were to recover from the depression. Perhaps they would find it difficult to have as their pastor someone who had experienced serious emotional problems.

Dr. Myer's story of his own depression had an encouraging conclusion. With the help of antidepressant medication and a skillful therapist, he gradually regained his emotional strength and self-confidence. Eventually he felt that he was ready to resume full-time ministry; yet he was uncertain how the members of his church would feel about him and his desire to return to the pulpit. But his doubts about their willingness to take him back as their pastor were erased as soon as he entered the sanctuary. He was greeted with applause and other expressions of approval and support. The church members loved him, and they wanted him back as their pastor.

Karen found Dr. Myer's story about his struggles with depression to be enlightening and encouraging. Perhaps there was hope for her if she would seek the same type of professional help he had sought. But it was another story Dr. Myer told that had the greatest impact on Karen. He told of an experience he had early in his career. He had noticed that a member of his congregation, a teenage girl, had not been in church for several Sundays. When he asked one of her friends about her, he was told that she had learned she was pregnant and had been sent by her parents to live with relatives in another community until she could have the baby and arrange for its adoption. Dr. Myer's immediate response was, "I wish I had known—I would have wanted to talk with her before she left." To which her friend responded, "Oh no, Rev. Myer, I'm sure you're the last person she would have wanted to see."

This comment hit him hard. He realized that something was seriously wrong with this view of the church and the ministry, and yet this was probably how many church members felt. During times when they felt like a failure and unworthy of the respect of others, the last person they wanted to see was their pastor. But this was completely contrary to Dr. Myer's vision of the church and his ministry. Pastors should be among the first individuals people turn to when they feel bad about themselves, and the church should be an institution they can look to for support during these times. Dr. Myer made a commitment to lead his church—and, he hoped, other churches—into alignment with this vision. His commitment and ability to articulate that vision gave Karen the courage to seek help in her own church.

At the end of the conference, as she sat in the sanctuary of College Park Baptist Church, Karen felt for the first time in months that it might be possible for her to find a path that would lead her out of her depression, and that one of the first stops along that path would be her church. Before she left, she promised herself that she would speak to her pastor after the worship service on Sunday and ask to meet with him to seek his support and guidance as she struggled with her depression. She also decided to make an appointment with her family physician to talk to him about what she had been experiencing and ask if he felt that one of the antidepressant medications she had learned about might prove helpful to her. Additionally, she would ask both her pastor and doctor for a recommendation about a psychotherapist.

Karen followed through with her plans. When she met with her pastor, she found that he listened attentively to everything she had to say and that he responded with words that indicated he genuinely understood what she was going through. She was surprised when he told her there were others in the congregation who had gone through similar experiences. And he was adamant that he did not view depression as a sign of weak faith or moral failure. He offered to pray with her and encouraged her to come back to see him whenever she felt she needed to talk. He also gave her the names of two psychotherapists he thought would be able to help her.

Karen's visit with her family physician also went well. After hearing the various symptoms she had been experiencing, he agreed with her assessment that she was clinically depressed and should be taking antidepressant medication. He talked to her about what she should expect from the medication. He cautioned her that she should not anticipate an immediate improvement in her mood. Antidepressant medications did not work that way. It could be three or four weeks, or maybe even a little longer, before she would notice significant changes. If the first medication he prescribed did not work, there were others they could try. He also informed her that there might be a few unwanted side effects; should she experience any, she needed to let him know. And he encouraged her not to rely solely on the medication. He wanted her to meet regularly with one of the psychotherapists her pastor had recommended.

Karen's path then led to a psychologist who was experienced in working with depression. Although it was her first time in psychotherapy, Karen felt comfortable talking about her problems, and the talking provided some relief. It felt good to speak openly and freely with someone who not only understood what she was going through, but could also offer helpful suggestions. She found the psychologist's calm demeanor and optimistic perspective on depression reassuring. There were no promises about a quick and easy recovery, but there were assurances that the combination of psychotherapy and antidepressant medication was effective for most people.

Having enlisted the help of her pastor, physician, and psychologist, Karen felt that she had made a good start on her journey out of depression. She was confident she was on the right path.

She was right. Within a month, Karen felt noticeably better. She felt she was gradually "coming back to life." Her body had lost some of its heaviness, in spite of the fact that her appetite had improved and she had gained a couple of pounds. She found it easier to laugh and joke with her children. Her concentration was improving. She could stay focused on her responsibilities at work and even enjoy reading again. Her positive thoughts about her husband and the marriage were now accompanied by positive feelings. And she found herself looking forward to Sunday mornings. Church was once again a place where she felt she belonged. The smiles and hugs from friends gave her strength, and the words of the prayers, hymns, and sermons reached deep into her heart and soul. Just three months after attending the conference on depression, she could happily report, "Life is good. Life is definitely worth living."

Koenig's Corner

Depression is common among those in religious congregations, albeit less common than in the general population. Aging, loss, and disappointments all have their impact, even on the most spiritually devout. A lot of misinformation concerning depression circulates around churches—that the person's faith is not strong enough, that he or she hasn't prayed or read the Bible or participated in religious activity enough. While religious activities can help to prevent the onset of depression and speed its recovery, the disorder itself often interferes with religious expression. Less severe depression may result in a deepening of religious faith and a coming closer to God. But severe depression actually blocks our access to God, results in a decrease in religious activity, and may propel the person to commit suicide. For that reason, church members must overcome the stigma that prevents many from obtaining necessary help. Instead, they must encourage loved ones and other church members with depression to get the help they need, rather than criticizing or questioning them about why they need to take medication or undergo psychotherapy. Karen felt alone and isolated. She needed education about her depression and permission to seek treatment. Education about the causes, course, and treatments of depression helps to combat misinformation, and there's no better place to educate church members than in the church itself.

Unfortunately, even many primary-care physicians are poorly trained in treating people with depression. Finding the right doctor may involve considerable effort. Happily, Karen had an unusually responsive physician. Furthermore, she also had a good deal of luck in finding a therapist she got along with and who effectively helped to guide her back to wellness. Just like physicians, therapists are not all alike, and patients should take care in choosing one who will understand and appreciate one's religious beliefs and values, as well as listen carefully.

Depression—Some Basic Information

- More than 18 million Americans suffer from depression.
- Women are twice as likely as men to experience depression.
- Depression is the number one risk factor for suicide.
- Women are more likely to attempt suicide, but men are four times more likely to actually commit suicide.
- The highest suicide rate is among elderly, white men.

- Depression can increase the risk of disability and death from other conditions because depressed individuals often lack the motivation to properly care for themselves.
- Depression is a highly treatable condition. The most widely used treatments are antidepressant medications and psychotherapy, or a combination of the two.

What Can Be Done in Your Congregation

- Provide information about the symptoms of depression:
  - depressed mood, feeling sad or empty
  - loss of interest or pleasure in activities previously enjoyed
  - significant change in weight or appetite
  - significant change in sleep patterns
  - restlessness or decrease in activity levels
  - fatigue or loss of energy
  - feelings of worthlessness, guilt, or hopelessness
  - difficulty thinking or concentrating, or indecisiveness
  - frequent thoughts of death or suicide
- Sponsor a program on depression featuring a psychiatrist, psychologist, or other mental health professional.
- Find ways to remove the stigma that is often attached to depression. Emphasize that depression should be treated as a medical condition and not as a sign of weakness or moral failure.
- Offer hope by providing information about the effective treatments for depression.
- Encourage members to talk to their personal physicians if they feel they might be depressed.

chapter ten

Answering the Call

What lessons can we learn from the experiences of the churches described in the preceding chapters? First and foremost, our times call out for churches to develop ministries of health and healing. The illnesses and serious health-related challenges presented in these chapters exist in every congregation and community right now, and in the coming years the number of people facing these and similar challenges will escalate dramatically. The future of the church in American society may rest on whether it responds to these challenges. If the church fails this test, then it faces the possibility of losing meaning to people who are dealing with very real day-to-day health problems—problems that church doctrines say Christians ought to be concerned about and involved in.

Another important lesson to be drawn from these stories is that it is possible for churches to develop meaningful health ministries without hiring additional staff or shifting financial resources away from other church programs. Although it would be wonderful if every church could hire a parish nurse, and hopefully many churches will, we know that many will not be able to. But this doesn't mean that every church can't have a health ministry. Within every congregation there are members who have the gifts of leadership and organization. In some churches, a retired educator may be eager to take the skills he or she developed in the classroom or an administrative position and put them to use again organizing a series of classes on health issues. In other churches, an individual who has developed an extensive social network that includes health professionals and feels comfortable asking for their assistance may be waiting to respond to a call for volunteers. Individuals such as these, given an appropriate understanding of the health needs of their congregations and the support of church leaders, can establish extraordinary and far-reaching health ministries. Every church has members who are known for their caring hearts, and many have the organizational skills to take the lead in establishing and sustaining a ministry. They are willing and eager to help, but they must be identified and informed.

What these accounts show to be essential to the development of a successful health ministry is the clear, unequivocal support of the clergy. In each of the programs cited in this book, leaders of the health ministries enjoyed the unwavering support and encouragement of their pastors. Unfortunately, we also know of churches in which the efforts of parish nurses and well-trained lay health educators failed because they did not have the sustained backing of their pastors.

It is important to understand, however, that saying the support of the clergy is crucial does not mean that pastors must take on additional time-consuming responsibilities. In fact, in many of the successful programs we have seen, the addition of a parish nurse or lay health ministry team provided some relief for the pastors. Even without the addition of a staff person, pastors do not need to be involved in the day-to-day operation of the ministry. What pastors must do is believe in the importance of the ministry, give their wholehearted support to it and to its leaders, and make that belief and that support known to the congregation in whatever ways they can. Pastors see the church from a perspective no one else has; and this perspective is what enables them to facilitate the integration of their health programs into the overall life of the church—without becoming involved themselves in the time-devouring minutiae of operation and without causing other ministries to suffer. It's primarily a matter of attitude and commitment: If pastors keep the vision alive in their own hearts and constantly before the people, success comes, as these accounts so clearly demonstrate.

We have also seen in our work that one of the reasons churches are able to develop health ministries, even if they are unable to add a parish nurse to their staff, is that medical institutions, including ones with no religious ties, are increasingly interested in collaborating with religious congregations. More and more physicians, nurses, health planners, and hospital administrators are recognizing the need for additional community-based health education and preventive medicine programs, and they are increasingly valuing the role that religion and spirituality can play in maintaining health as the research literature demonstrating this continues to grow. They know that people throughout their communities need more information about illness prevention and disease management, along with easier access to screenings and basic medical services. One way they can efficiently and effectively take these resources out into their communities is by working in partnership with religious congregations.

Additionally, we have seen that within many churches there are physicians and other health care providers who welcome the chance to participate in congregational health ministries. They enjoy having the opportunity to teach and discuss medical topics in a church setting, and they find that it is an ideal way for them to bring together the two healing traditions of which they are a part.

Another encouraging development we have witnessed is the ability of churches to work across denominational lines to establish health ministries. Many of the issues that create deep divisions among Christians seem to recede into the background when church members focus on meeting the health needs of their congregations and communities. They have seen how effective their ministries of health and healing can be when they work together.

One of the most encouraging and gratifying aspects of our work with these churches has been to see the impact of health ministries on the parish nurses and volunteers who have been actively involved in these programs. Parish nurses find that these programs enable them to deliver the whole-person care that they have always wanted to provide. They are able to attend to the spiritual, psychological, and social dimensions as well as the physical dimension of individuals facing serious medical problems. Many have commented on how much more rewarding it is to practice "high touch" rather than "high tech" nursing.

For church volunteers with no previous training or experience in health care, the opportunity to acquire the knowledge and resources that allow them to serve as instruments of healing has been a transforming experience. We have heard so many of these Christians say that for years they had felt called to reach out and help people facing serious health problems, but they had often felt powerless to respond to individuals in need. The training they received in these programs, however, finally gave them the ability to participate directly in a ministry of health and healing, and they were grateful for the opportunity to put their faith into practice in this meaningful way.

There is no question that altruism has been the primary motivation of the volunteers who have participated in and contributed to health ministry programs. They have given their time and energy because they want to serve God by serving others, and they have felt richly rewarded by seeing so many people benefit from their work. But a number of the volunteers have told us that they also discovered an unexpected benefit for themselves. They found that the information they were given about a certain illness or treatment or community resource later proved to be valuable when they themselves became ill or when a loved one developed a serious health problem. They were able to confront their own health-related challenges with greater confidence and peace of mind because they understood the nature of the problem and knew where to turn for help. Although their motivation for volunteering for health ministry programs had not been to benefit themselves, they had, in fact, derived valuable personal benefits. And research is showing that those benefits include not only a greater sense of purpose and meaning in life, but also measurably better physical health and greater longevity as well.

The churches we have reported on in this book, along with hundreds of others across the country, have found marvelous ways to extend the healing ministry of Jesus to their congregations and communities. They have been able to do so because pastors and committed members have understood and responded to the needs and opportunities that exist in all our communities. We have been greatly inspired by what we have seen and heard from both the leaders of these health ministries and those whose lives have been touched by these programs. We hope that their stories will inspire other Christians to develop similar health ministries and thus help the church reclaim its historical role as a healing institution.

appendix

Resources for Ministries of Health and Healing

Institute for Congregational and Community Health

Stetson University
Campus Box 8272
DeLand, FL 32723
(386) 822-7289
www.stetson.edu/icch

The mission of the Institute for Congregational and Community Health is to promote the development of faith-based programs that address the health needs of religious congregations and the communities they serve. The institute offers workshops and consultation services and provides materials to help religious congregations and hospitals develop and sustain health ministries. The institute also works closely with the Center for Community Health Ministry at Florida Hospital to support its training programs.

Center for Community Health Ministry

Florida Hospital
2400 Bedford Road, 2nd Floor
Orlando, FL 32803
(407) 303-5574
www.parishnursing.net

The Center for Community Health Ministry is committed to working with all communities, faiths, and denominations that wish to begin developing a health ministry. Hospitals wishing to begin developing this method of outreach to their communities can contact the center for consultation and Coordinator Preparation Training Programs. Ongoing classes for congregations include:

Parish Nurse Basic Preparation Course—an eight-day intensive training that uses the standardized curriculum approved by the International Parish Nurse Resource Center and recommended by the American Nurses Association.

Lay Health Education Class—a twelve-hour class that prepares members of the health ministry cabinet or team to begin a health ministry.

Lay Health Advocacy Class—a twelve-hour class that prepares members of the health ministry cabinet or team to understand the elements of advocacy ministry.

Center for the Study of Religion/Spirituality and Health

Box 3400 Duke University Medical Center
Durham, NC 27710
(919) 681-6633
www.dukespiritualityandhealth.org

The purpose of the Center for the Study of Religion/Spirituality and Health is to conduct multidisciplinary research on the effects of religion or spirituality on physical and mental health. Center faculty members are interested in working with clergy, theologians, and other scientists to learn more about how religion affects health as well as explore the medical and theological implications of its effects. Center faculty members often give presentations on religion and health to outside groups.

Caring Communities Program

Duke Divinity School
3600 University Drive, Suite D
Durham, NC 27707
(919) 401-3737 ext. 102
www.divinity.duke.edu

The Caring Communities Program was created to invest in the communities of the Carolinas by supporting the development and sustenance of health ministries programs through the work of the Health Ministries Resource Center. In keeping with that mission, the program seeks to nurture practices of caring that embody faithfulness, gratitude, and hospitality within communities; develop and systematically implement a curriculum of spirituality and health; systematically assess the practices of health ministry; and establish the Carolinas as a leader in health ministries and health care innovation.

Health Ministries Association

980 Canton Street
Building 1, Suite B
Roswell, GA 30075
(800) 280-9919
www.hmassoc.org

The Health Ministries Association is an interfaith membership organization, serving the people who serve the Faith Health Ministry Movement. The mission of the HMA is to encourage, support, and develop whole-person ministries leading to the integration of faith and health. HMA's vision for the future is to establish the integration of faith and health as an essential part of the United States health system.

Shepherd's Hope

4851 S. Apopka-Vineland Road
Orlando, FL 32819
(407) 876-6699
www.shepherdshope.org

Shepherd's Hope is a nonprofit faith-based organization providing free medical care for low-income, uninsured men, women, and children who do not have access to needed medical care. Shepherd's Hope, in partnership with its sponsoring churches, operates health care centers located on school or church campuses that are open in the evenings and staffed entirely by volunteers.

Share the Care

808 West Central Boulevard
Orlando, FL 32805
(407) 423-5311

Share the Care is a nondenominational, nonprofit organization specializing in adult day care and respite for frail elderly adults and individuals with Alzheimer's disease. Share the Care offers a wide range of services, including case management, in-home counseling, adult day centers, in-home respite care, crisis care, overnight care in assisted-living facilities, and a memory disorder clinic.

Life Line Screening

5400 Transportation Boulevard
Cleveland, OH 44125
(800) 449-2350
www.lifelinescreening.com

Life Line Screening provides noninvasive, painless screenings using Doppler ultrasound technology. Life Line Screening has mobile units and personnel throughout the continental United States and can arrange to conduct screening events in churches and other houses of worship.

Wheat Ridge Ministries

One Pierce Place, Suite 250E
Itasca, IL 60143
(800) 762-6748
www.wheatridge.org

Wheat Ridge Ministries is an independent Lutheran charitable organization that provides support for new church-related health and hope ministries. It is a recognized service organization of the Lutheran Church-Missouri Synod and an affiliated social ministry organization of the Evangelical Lutheran Church in America. Reflecting Christ's concern for the whole person (John 10:10), Wheat Ridge Ministries is committed to seeding new and innovative ministries that focus on health of body, mind, and spirit.

Grants from Wheat Ridge Ministries have supported the work of Shepherd's Hope (see chapter 2) and the Health Ministry Team at Trinity Lutheran Church (see chapter 3).

Faith in Action

A National Program of The Robert Wood Johnson Foundation
Wake Forest University School of Medicine
Medical Center Boulevard
Winston-Salem, NC 27157
(877) 324-8411
www.fiavolunteers.org

Faith in Action is an interfaith volunteer caregiving program of The Robert Wood Johnson Foundation. Faith in Action makes grants to local groups representing many faiths who volunteer to work together to care for their neighbors who have long-term illnesses or disabilities. The foundation has committed $100 million to expand the Faith in Action national movement. In addition to providing start-up grants, the national office offers Faith in Action programs support and advice on developing successful, sustainable caregiving programs.

Grants from Faith in Action have supported programs of Share the Care (see chapter 5).

Local Initiative Funding Partners

A National Program Office of The Robert Wood Johnson Foundation
760 Alexander Road
P. O. Box 1
Princeton, NJ 08543
(609) 275-4128
www.lifp.org

The Local Initiative Funding Partners program is a partnership between The Robert Wood Johnson Foundation and local grant makers that supports innovative, community-based projects to improve health and health care for underserved and at-risk populations. Local Initiative Funding Partners provides grants of $100,000 to $500,000 per project, which must be matched dollar for dollar by local grant makers such as community foundations, family foundations, corporations, and others.

It was through Local Initiative Funding Partners that Shepherd's Hope (see chapter 2) received a four-year matching grant from The Robert Wood Johnson Foundation. The Dr. P. Phillips Foundation served as the local funding partner.